The Case for
Medicare for All

T0087467

Gerald Friedman

———

The Case for Medicare for All

polity

First published in 2020 by Polity Press

Polity Press
65 Bridge Street
Cambridge CB2 1UR, UK

Polity Press
101 Station Landing
Suite 300
Medford, MA 02155, USA

ISBN-13: 978-1-5095-3976-5
ISBN-13: 978-1-5095-3977-2 (pb)

A catalogue record for this book is available from the British Library.

Typeset in 11 on 15 Sabon by Servis Filmsetting Ltd, Stockport, Cheshire
Printed and bound in the UK by TJ International Limited

For further information on Polity, visit our website: politybooks.com

Contents

Figures and Tables

Figures and Tables

Acknowledgements

Over the years, I have benefited from advice and guidance from Leonard Rodberg, Michael Ash, Ben Day, Peter Arno, Michael Dukakis, Erin Georgen, Ida Hellender, Betty Johnson, Lawrence King, Ted Levy, Richard Master, Lee Mercer, Sam Metz, Ivan Miller, Stephanie Nakajima, Eric Naumberg, Chuck Pennacchio, Frank Puig, Katie Robbins, Len Rodberg, Debbie Silverstein, Mark Stelzner, Chris Sturr, Ed Weisbart, and Ralph Whitehead. Len Rodberg, Larry King, and Joe Kane gave an earlier draft a careful reading for which I am most grateful; Debra Jacobson read the penultimate draft and made very helpful edits and suggestions. Students Tiffany Duong, Joe Kane, Joshua Weinstein, and, especially, Tai Spargo-Pasquini, have provided invaluable assistance, as well as advice. I am most

Acknowledgements

grateful to my editors at Polity, George Owers and Julia Davies. Polity's five anonymous referees were helpful beyond my wildest hopes, for which I am very grateful. They were all thoughtful and constructive; referees one and three even provided a line by line review. All can take a share of whatever is worthwhile here; none are responsible for the opinions expressed or remaining errors.

In my work on behalf of Medicare for All I have spoken in more than a dozen states to over 100 groups. All have provided intellectual stimulation and inspiration. This book is intended to help my many many friends in their work, and I dedicate it to all those good people that I have met along the way. And, of course, it is for Debra, who has been my companion every step, and remains my guiding light.

Preface: We Need Better

This little book reflects the concerns and struggles that have preoccupied my life. When I turned 13, in that explosive year 1968, I imagined that we were on the cusp of a new era of social reform. Liberal Democrats like Hubert Humphrey seemed lame, lacking ambition at a time when social movements were moving far beyond the welfare state towards true economic democracy, a world where we would treat everyone with respect and compassion, "from each according to their ability, to each according to their needs."

I have not changed my values, but 50 years have taught me political humility. The opposition we face is much stronger and our revolutionary social movements much weaker than had seemed to be the case in that turbulent year. I have learned that we need to be much smarter, and more political. We need to cultivate allies, even among those who may not agree with our ultimate goals. And we need to use those alliances to build institutions that create experiences capable of allaying fears. Already in college at Columbia University and graduate school at Harvard University, I looked for clues from the successful social movements: the bourgeois revolutionaries, the abolitionists, and the labor movements of the twentieth century. My earlier works studied these. That is the background and experience that I bring to bear here.

The campaign for universal healthcare in America is a century old. Reformers have made the case intellectually but have failed because they have not unraveled the politics. That is my task in this book: to go beyond the economic case for Medicare for All to address this political issue. What do we need to do to win? Where might we seek allies? How might we disarm the opposition? How might we build state institutions to prepare for Medicare for All while allaying fears and building public support? Truly, lives depend on our success in answering such questions.

Introduction: The Failure of Free Market Healthcare

Killed By For-Profit Healthcare

Alec Smith died on June 27, 2017, less than a month after turning 26. While his death certificate lists diabetic ketoacidosis as the cause of death, he was killed by the health insurance industry. He developed diabetes three years before his death, and his condition was treated very effectively with insulin, a product developed over a century ago by Frederick Banting and other Canadian scientists who donated the patent to the world so that no one should be denied this life-saving medication.[1]

For 80 years, insulin was widely available because the lack of patent protection allowed many companies to produce competing generic varieties. In the 1980s, however, new and improved insulin versions were developed, innovations that made insulin a little safer and more effective, while also giving drug companies the opportunity to patent variants and an incentive to stop producing the older, less profitable generic insulin. There are now only three companies producing insulin, and they are ruthlessly exploiting their market power to profit off the 30 million Americans with diabetes. In the last few years, insulin prices have soared, increasing by nearly 300%, from an average price of $4.34 per milliliter in 2002 to $12.92 per milliliter in 2013.[2] Prices in the United States are much higher than elsewhere; many Canadians and Europeans pay barely one-sixth of what Americans pay.[3] In late 2017, Humalog, a fast-acting insulin, cost $115 in the United States versus $20 in Canada, almost a six-fold markup.[4] Unless we are to believe that the manufacturer was selling at a loss in Canada out of a charitable impulse towards Canadian diabetics, then we can only conclude that the manufacturer, Eli Lilly, is making a lot of money off diabetics in the United States.

To cope with rising prices, diabetics resort to "self-rationing," stretching out their supplies, often with toxic results. For Alec Smith, the high cost of insulin was literally deadly. When he aged out of his parents' health insurance at age 26, he was working in a restaurant job that did not provide health insurance. Because he earned too much to qualify for Medicaid or other public assistance, he looked to buy a health insurance policy on the Minnesota insurance exchange. Even with a government subsidy, a decent health insurance plan cost much more than he could afford on his restaurant salary. The only policy he could find had a $7600 deductible, which he would have to pay before the insurance company would help him pay the $1300 a month for his insulin. Passing on an insurance plan that would not help him for at least six months, Smith planned to pay for his insulin out-of-pocket. Without ready cash to pay for another dose, he tried to stretch out his supply to make it until his next paycheck. He did not make it.

Alec Smith did not have health insurance, but many with insurance fare no better. Health insurance companies refer to the money they pay out in benefits, money spent on healthcare, as "medical losses"—expenses to be minimized whenever possible. Shane Patrick Boyle discovered one way in which insurers limit their losses. Moving from his Texas home to Arkansas to help his ailing mother, he found that his Texas plan did not cover insulin purchased out-of-state. Instead of leaving his mother and driving back to his Texas pharmacy to renew his prescription, Boyle thought he could stretch out his supply while he scrambled for money to buy insulin out-of-pocket. He died $50 short of the $750 he needed.[5]

Shane Boyle posted an appeal on GoFundMe. com for charitable contributions to help him buy insulin. Millions like him have gone to charity sites for help paying for insulin or other essential medical care. Some have succeeded; most do not.[6] Audi, a cute five-year-old, was able to raise over $2000 for a new insulin pump. Makayla Sterner, despite posting a sweet picture of her with her toddler son, was only able to raise half of the $1500 she needed for an insulin pump when, even after multiple blackouts, her insurance company told her it was not medically necessary. Still, she did better than Micaela Archibald. Only 11 people donated to her campaign for a pump, a drive that raised only 10% of what she needed.

GoFundMe.com was started as a crowdfunding site to raise funds for "ideas and dreams," "wedding donations and honeymoon registry." Most collection efforts from the first year were "related to such . . . special occasions." A category for medical needs existed, but it was further down the list. Now, however, there are nearly 250,000 medical appeals per year, raising a third of the $5 billion collected on the site—a symptom. Rob Solomon, the site's founder, concludes that "the healthcare system in the United States is really broken."[7]

> The government is supposed to be there and sometimes they are. The healthcare companies are supposed to be there and sometimes they are. But for literally millions of people they're not. The only thing you can really do is rely on the kindness of friends and family and community. That's where GoFundMe comes in. I was not ready for that at all when I started at the company.[8]

Is this how we want to pay for healthcare?

Medicare for All?

We have been debating healthcare for a century. I have been involved in the debate for nearly half that time, ever since I took a bus from New York to Washington DC in 1977 to lobby for Senator Ted Kennedy's single-payer proposal. Kennedy's bill failed, inaugurating a period where reform proposals grew less and less ambitious even while the problems in our healthcare system grew more acute. From the 1980s through the Affordable Care Act of 2010, Democrats began each cycle by accepting the last conservative proposal even while Republicans moved further away from any concept of government-funded universal healthcare.[9] When the Democrats finally enacted a serious reform, the Affordable Care Act, it drew on legislation enacted by a Republican governor, Mitt Romney of Massachusetts, based on a 1994 proposal by Republican Senators John Chafee and Robert Dole.

This dynamic of Democrats chasing Republicans to the right changed abruptly in 2016 when Vermont Senator Bernie Sanders made universal coverage the centerpiece of his campaign for the Democratic presidential nomination against Hillary Clinton. Sanders moved Medicare for All to the center of American politics. After a decade where there had not even been a Medicare for All proposal in the Senate, Sanders filed a bill in 2015 without a single cosponsor. When he refiled in 2017, there were 16 cosponsors and the leading Medicare for All bill in the House of Representatives, filed by Representative Jayapal of Washington state, has over 110 cosponsors.

Medicare for All has arrived, but with a misleading title. While varying in detail, both the Senate and House bills are substantially different from existing Medicare. Financed with a mixture of payroll taxes, premiums, and extensive cost-sharing,

Medicare provides a narrow range of health benefits, requiring seniors to rely on wraparound insurance plans or Medicaid to cover the rest.[10] By contrast, both Medicare for All proposals are comprehensive, including pharmaceutical, dental, vision, and long-term care. Without cost-sharing, co-pays, deductibles, and without limits on benefits, they would largely negate any need for private insurance.[11] They also differ in the funding mechanism. While Medicare relies on trust funds fed by payroll taxes, the Sanders and Jayapal Medicare for All programs would be funded on a pay-as-you-go basis, relying on new income or other taxes.

In short, Medicare for All proposals do not extend Medicare to all Americans, they create a new program, more comprehensive, but like Medicare in one crucial way: benefits are paid by the federal government.

Medicare for All proposals are also distinguished from those designed to build on the current insurance system by improving existing Medicare or opening it to the general public.[12] While the latter programs would increase the share of the public with health insurance, by preserving the current for-profit private insurance system they would maintain many of the restrictions on access that killed Alec Smith and Shane Boyle. Furthermore, by maintaining the fragmented insurance system, they would limit the types of financial savings possible only with the single-payer system. Finally, while Medicare for All would shift the burden of paying for healthcare to the ability to pay through general taxation, these other programs would continue to rely on premiums and cost-sharing, maintaining the burden on low- and moderate-income households.

This book outlines the economic case for an improved Medicare for All like that proposed by Sanders and Jayapal. But it is about politics as well as economics. After discussing the problems with the current system and demonstrating the viability of an improved Medicare for All system, the book shows how we can move forward with interim steps and alliances to build popular support. The key is to introduce measures that create the infrastructure for Medicare for All while demonstrating how government can contribute to a better and more efficient healthcare system. What we need are revolutionary reforms that build Medicare for All, not patches on a failing system.

The Failure of Free Market Healthcare

How Well Does the United States Provide Healthcare?

The American system of for-profit insurance and medicine is unique among affluent countries, and it clearly does not work well. Elsewhere, governments fund a much larger share of health expenditures than in the United States and regulate private insurance very closely. Everywhere else, most healthcare is paid for out of tax revenue and is provided either by government agencies (such as the British National Health Service) or by highly regulated private bodies.[13]

From this perspective, the United States has been conducting a social experiment in health policy, testing whether it is possible to provide quality healthcare efficiently and equitably when directed by private individuals and entities dedicated to profit making. If that was the intention, we can now drop the experiment because the answer is clearly "no": for-profit medicine is not only inequitable but also inefficient. By virtually every metric, healthcare in the United States is much more expensive than elsewhere and distributed with much greater disparities. In Bloomberg's healthy country index, the United States ranked 35 in 2018, behind much poorer countries like Cuba, Slovenia, and Chile and

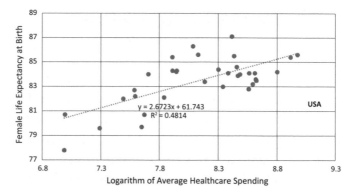

Figure 1: Female life expectancy at birth and per capita healthcare expenditures, 2016, OECD countries and the United States

Note: This figure shows the relationship between female life expectancy and the logarithm of per capita healthcare expenditures for member states within the Organisation for Economic Co-operation and Development (OECD). The line shown is the average relationship between these two for member states other than the United States. The position of the United States well below and to the right of the line indicates that it is spending much more than other countries but has significantly shorter female life expectancy than would be expected given this level of spending.

one place below its rank of 34 in 2017.[14] The World Health Organization similarly ranks the United States at 37 out of 191 countries, above Slovenia but behind Dominica and Costa Rica, not to mention France or Italy (rated 1 and 2 respectively).[15] Furthermore, the US is sinking in the rankings, as its privatized healthcare system has been getting relatively worse.

The Failure of Free Market Healthcare

The point of healthcare spending is improved health and to extend life. On that basis, healthcare in the United States, while much better than it was in the past, has fallen behind other countries. We would expect affluence to bring greater longevity because of better nutrition and more comfortable lifestyles. For the same reason, we would expect life expectancy to *increase* over time as countries grow richer and are better able to provide quality nutrition, clean water, and improved healthcare.

Growing affluence has been associated with longer average national life expectancy, but much less so for the United States (see Figure 2). Among the world's wealthiest nations, we are less healthy than many poorer countries. Despite our affluence, our health outcomes were already below average in 1971; and, while we are living longer and healthier lives now, improvement has been much slower than elsewhere, slower than would be expected given our increasing wealth. While women in the US live 6.2 years longer now than in 1971, Canadian women live 7.5 years longer, British women 7.8 years longer, and French women 9.6 years longer.[16] Since 1971, the United States has dropped from 19th to 34th place among members of the Organisation for Economic Co-operation and Development (OECD) in potential years of

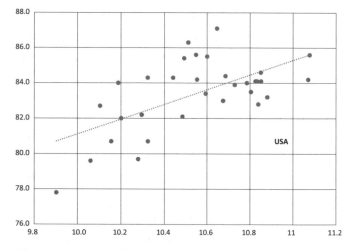

Figure 2: Female life expectancy and the logarithm of per capita income, OECD, 2016

Note: This figure shows the relationship between female life expectancy and the logarithm of per capita income for member states within the OECD. The line shown is the average relationship between these two for member states other than the United States. The position of the United States well below and to the right of the line indicates that life expectancy in the US is about four years less than would be expected given its income level. Indeed, the US has shorter female life expectancy than most affluent countries.

female life lost (see Table 1). One reason for our poor health performance is that we have a higher infant mortality rate than 30 of 35 OECD members. Indeed, having children in the United States is particularly risky. At 14 deaths per 100,000 live births, the US maternal mortality rate is the worst in the affluent world, not only twice the rate

Table 1: US healthcare in comparative perspective

Measure		Share of OECD Countries Performing Better Than the US
Potential years of life lost, all causes, years lost/100,000 males, aged 0–69 years	1971	71%
	2016	82%
Potential years of life lost, all causes, years lost/100,000 females, aged 0–69 years	1971	79%
	2016	97%
Infant mortality rate	1971	50%
	2016	91%
Life expectancy, male, at birth	1971	56%
	2016	74%
Life expectancy, female, at birth	1971	37%
	2016	83%

Note: This table shows the standing of the United States compared to other member states of the OECD in 1971 and 2016 for various measures of healthcare performance. In every measure, the United States now performs worse relative to other affluent countries than it did in 1971.

in Canada and triple that in Japan, but twice the rate in the relatively poor countries of Croatia, Slovakia, and Slovenia.[17]

Since the United States has many of the world's best doctors and the most advanced medical technology, it is surprising that Americans die at such high rates. The problem is that our healthcare finance system blocks many from access to even basic healthcare, and forces doctors and nurses to waste excessive time and energy dealing with a recalcitrant financing system designed to maximize profit rather than health. Much of the discussion over the last decades has been about those like Alec Smith without any health insurance.[18] A study of cancer treatments explains this in cold clinical terms: "In the absence of health insurance coverage, many forgo cancer screening and/ or delay diagnosis and thus are likely to experience poor clinical outcomes."[19] Health insurance, however, does not guarantee access to healthcare. Restrictions on access have become increasingly burdensome for many with insurance, like Shane Boyle. A recent survey found that while almost all diabetics had health insurance, 40% had rationed test strips and 26% had rationed insulin over the past year.[20]

Private health insurers have made rationing worse with a range of tools designed to inflate profits by limiting access to healthcare services. Benefits are conditional on the use of doctors and services selected by insurance companies, with financial penalties for those who use services outside of narrow networks or without prior authorization. Almost 90% of Americans with private health insurance now face deductibles, the minimum spending required before benefits begin. Since 2008, the average deductible has more than doubled, reaching almost $2000 in policies covering individuals and $3400 in policies covering families. Virtually all insurance plans now cover expenses only after a co-pay, or payment by the patient before the insurance company pays anything. Co-payments for office visits average around $25, and for hospital admissions over $300 per day.[21]

Since many Americans do not have significant available cash to cover emergencies, with almost half not having even $400 to hand, mounting cost-sharing forces them to choose between medical care and other essential bills.[22] Doctors complain of patients who risk their health by not following recommended medication regimens or seeking follow-up care, but such "noncompliance" is a result of tragic financial constraints rather than an irresponsible act of defiance. The Federal Reserve finds that over 25% of Americans have skipped medical care because of cost. These noncompliant patients risk "adverse clinical outcomes" because they cannot afford the care they need.[23] Their financial situation is more toxic than their disease.

Together, foregone treatment and medication nonadherence kill thousands, even hundreds of thousands, of Americans. This is demonstrated in a comparison of the share of a county's population

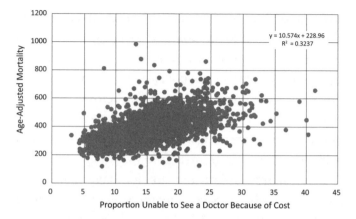

Figure 3: Lack of access to healthcare and mortality, counties in the United States, 2015

Note: This figure shows for over 3000 counties in the United States the relationship between the proportion who reported they could not see a doctor because of cost and the county's age-adjusted mortality. The line shown is the average relationship between the two; the upward slope indicates that a higher proportion of people die in counties where more people report they cannot afford to see a doctor.

who report that they could not afford to see a doctor when sick with that county's age-adjusted mortality rate (see Figure 3). No one should be surprised that the larger the share unable to afford a doctor, the higher the mortality rate; indeed, this alone accounts for nearly a third of the variation in county mortality rates in the United States. Much of the excess mortality in the United States compared with other affluent countries can be associated with financial barriers to access, and most of these excess deaths are of people *with* health insurance.[24] Measured in crass economic terms, if we value human lives at $9 million apiece, as is done by the Environmental Protection Agency, the annual economic cost of this excess mortality could be in the hundreds of billions of dollars.

The Rising Cost of Our Poor-Quality Healthcare

Ironically, efforts to restrain healthcare spending by restricting access have failed catastrophically to restrain costs even while killing Americans. Americans pay much more for healthcare than do residents of other countries, and the gap has grown over the past decades while health insurers have been restricting access to care. Healthcare spending in the United States, about $10,000 per person, is twice as much as in the rest of the OECD. Spending has also risen faster in the US: since 1971, it has increased as a share of gross domestic product nearly twice as fast as in the rest of the OECD. We might be happy to pay this price if it came with commensurate improvements in healthcare, but, as mentioned above, our life expectancy gains have been among the lowest in the OECD. We have paid nearly $1300 per person for every one-year increase in life expectancy since 1971, triple the price paid in the rest of the OECD ($399 per person). At this rate, to equal the life expectancy of other affluent countries, we would have to raise our spending to over $14,000 per person, almost triple the average of other affluent OECD countries.

This $9000 margin per person per year—the gap between what we would need to spend to reach the same life expectancy as other countries and what they actually spend—is one measure of the dollar cost of our inefficient healthcare finance system.

The rising cost of healthcare is interfering with everything else that we try to do. Instead of raising wages, employers have been paying more and more for their workers' rising health insurance costs. Real spending on private health insurance per employee has soared since 2007, absorbing an additional $5000 per employee in family plans—money unavailable to pay workers so that they can pay for housing, vacations, schooling for their children, or to put food on the table. From 2007 to 2014, healthcare spending by middle-class households climbed by 25% even while spending on housing fell by 6%, on food by 8%, and on clothing by 19% (see Figure 4).[25] The rising cost of healthcare

The Failure of Free Market Healthcare

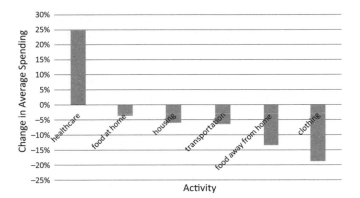

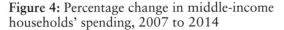

Figure 4: Percentage change in middle-income households' spending, 2007 to 2014

Note: This figure shows the change in real spending for middle-income households on healthcare and other activities from 2007 to 2014. While healthcare spending has risen, spending on all other activities has fallen.

is not only killing Americans and undermining their children's education, it is also bankrupting them. Around 20% of Americans had medical debt in 2014, leading in too many cases to bankruptcy. Nearly a million Americans went bankrupt in 2017, and as many as 60% of these bankruptcies were due to medical debt.[26] Over half a million bankruptcies is a steep price to pay for private health insurance.

It does not have to be this way. Americans certainly know that they pay more for healthcare; growing numbers, nearly 2 million in 2019, go abroad for care, and as many as 19 million buy medications abroad.[27] It is estimated that the medical tourism market is growing by 25% a year, with the top destinations being Costa Rica, Mexico, India, and Southeast Asia.[28] We can make a direct comparison of the cost of our private, for-profit health insurance system by looking across the border at Canada, which has operated a public health insurance program for nearly half a century, and where the process of healthcare, the way doctors treat patients, is quite similar to the United States.[29] With publicly funded universal coverage, Canadian healthcare spending has increased at a much slower rate even while Canadians receive more healthcare and live longer than do their neighbors in the United States. Healthcare in Canada is so much more efficient than in the United States that if we used healthcare services at the Canadian rate—if we went to the doctor as often, used as many prescription drugs, and had hospital stays as long—then US healthcare spending would cost 70% more: an additional $7000 per person or nearly 24% of national income.

The difference is that Canadians pay lower prices for their healthcare services. They get more healthcare for less money because their system is better at promoting efficiency while controlling prices.[30]

Changing Policy: From Campaigning for Universal Coverage to Medicare

As mentioned earlier, Americans have been debating how to pay for healthcare for over a century. In 1912, Theodore Roosevelt's Progressive Party called for "[t]he protection of home life against the hazards of sickness, irregular employment and old age through the adoption of a system of social insurance adapted to American use."[31] Roosevelt's Progressives lost the 1912 election but his cousin, Franklin D. Roosevelt, incorporated many of Theodore's ideas into his New Deal. In 1935, FDR's Committee on Economic Security recommended that a "national program of economic security would be inadequate unless it made adequate provision against insecurity arising out of illness," because "tens of millions of families live in dread of sickness" which forces them to sacrifice "essentials of decent living in order to pay for medical service," "go without needed medical care," or "carry the burden of medical debts."[32]

The Committee recommended federal funding of public health insurance, but opposition from the American Medical Association (AMA), among others, led FDR to drop a health program from the legislation that eventually established our Social

21

Security system. Healthcare, he promised, would be treated separately later. Roosevelt returned to healthcare, proposing in his 1944 State of the Union address, for example, an Economic Bill of Rights including the "right to adequate medical care."[33] While it formed the basis of the G.I. Bill of Rights and veterans' healthcare, public insurance for the general public was again deferred in the face of opposition from the AMA, private health insurers, and others. In 1945, President Truman renewed the Roosevelts' campaign for national health insurance, and won reelection in 1948 on the issue. But again, it did not happen.

This repeated failure of campaigns for universal public provision has had lasting political consequences. The lack of a public program has fostered the development of private interests whose benefits, and profits, would be threatened by such a program. Already when Theodore Roosevelt proposed a national system, some employers had begun to offer health insurance to win workers' loyalty and encourage longer job tenure.[34] Looking to promote coverage without raising taxes or pushing a program through a recalcitrant Congress, FDR supported the spread of employer-provided insurance plans, even introducing a backdoor subsidy through a tax exemption for income given as health insurance. Without a national plan, many unions opted to join in by negotiating for employer-provided health insurance plans. Some even saw expensive private health insurance as a way of pushing employers to join in the campaign for universal public provision.[35]

Defeated in campaigns for universal health insurance, liberals tried a new tack, offering partial public coverage, beginning with the elderly, in order to demonstrate the feasibility of national insurance while building the infrastructure for a universal program. The idea was to begin with a group enjoying extensive public sympathy, but with little private health insurance, and then extend the program to children and others until, ultimately, universal coverage was reached. As one of the originators of the new approach, and architect of our Social Security system, Robert Ball, wrote decades later:

all of us who developed Medicare and fought for it . . . had been advocates of universal national health insurance. We all saw insurance for the elderly as a fallback position, which we advocated solely because it seemed to have the best chance politically. Although the public record contains some explicit denials, we expected Medicare to be a first step toward universal national health insurance, perhaps with "Kiddicare" as another step.[36]

23

Medicare and Medicaid

As Ball suggests, liberals did not give up on national health insurance. The Democratic platform in 1960 proclaimed a "right to adequate medical care," before focusing on "our older citizens" for whom the problem of inadequate health insurance "is particularly acute" and "among whom serious illness strikes most often." For them, if not yet for anyone else, the convention that nominated John Fitzgerald Kennedy for the presidency promised: "we shall provide medical care benefits for the aged as part of the time-tested Social Security insurance system."[37]

It took a struggle, and another presidential election, to enact Medicare in 1965, providing health insurance coverage for the elderly along with a new Medicaid program covering the poor (including many of the elderly). Ball and his allies pushed to extend this opening. Legislation in 1972 extended Medicare to cover those with long-term disabilities as well as those with certain diseases. Today, nearly 20% of Americans are covered by Medicare, at a cost substantially lower than that of providing coverage through private insurance. The program has contributed to a dramatic improvement in the lives of the elderly and the disabled, with a substantial increase in life expectancy for the former, and especially the very old.[38] Relative to their counterparts in other affluent countries, elderly Americans are significantly healthier than younger Americans. The life expectancy gap between residents of the United States and those living in other countries peaks right before the eligibility age for Medicare and then narrows significantly. By their eighties, Americans can expect to live as long as people in Canada. Medicare works on both sides of the 49th parallel.

For a few years in the 1970s it seemed that Ball's strategy would bear fruit, with the only remaining issue being the choice between a completely public program and one with space remaining for private health insurance.[39] But after the extension of Medicare to the disabled in 1972, little progress was made for nearly 40 years. With Democrats abandoning Ball's vision of universally available social insurance and accepting Republican proposals, measures to gain universal access were repeatedly beaten back. The breakthrough came in 2010 when the Patient Protection and Affordable Care Act (ACA) was enacted after a Herculean struggle.[40] The first significant expansion of public healthcare coverage in nearly half a century, the ACA introduced significant reforms of private health insurance. These included regulations to prevent some of the insurers' worst practices, a major expansion of the Medicaid system for the poor, and the establishment of simplified healthcare marketplaces. While the ACA did not expand health insurance to cover all Americans, it did reverse a 20-year trend of decline by extending coverage to over 20 million additional people through a mix of Medicaid expansion and subsidies to help low- and middle-income Americans purchase private health insurance.[41] Regulatory reforms, such as forbidding denial of coverage for pre-existing conditions, were also often major boons for less healthy Americans.[42] Financed with a tax on high-income households and reductions in the overpayment for private Medicare Advantage plans, the bill also marked a major redistribution towards low- and middle-income households.[43]

Most on the left, and virtually all Democrats, defend the ACA for these accomplishments. Yet few have been enthusiastic.[44] Tens of millions are still without insurance, and the coverage provided has been disappointing. The ACA pegs subsidies to the cost of so-called "silver" insurance plans, whose actuarial value—the share of medical expenses covered—is only 70%. By limiting the cost to the insurance company, a low actuarial value limits the cost of government subsidies, at the expense of subscribers who, on average, face deductibles of over $4000.[45] Worse, the rising cost of healthcare is driving up these deductibles and the price of other forms of cost-sharing in both ACA plans and all other forms of private health insurance. Despite a plethora of measures intended to control costs by tweaking payment methods and coverage provisions, the ACA has largely failed to control rising costs beyond the continuing efforts of insurers to lower them by discouraging utilization through rising cost-sharing. The Centers for Medicare and Medicaid Services (CMS) now projects that healthcare spending will rise by over 5% a year for the next decade—significantly faster than income.[46]

As critics predicted at the time, the ACA has failed to maintain affordability because it did not address the real cost drivers pushing up US healthcare spending: the drive for profits, and the inefficiency this produces in our fragmented private healthcare system. Rather than build a popular movement to force Congressional action, the law's architects secured its passage by trading away measures that threatened major stakeholders, drug companies, insurers, and hospitals. The ACA experience demonstrates, however, that the only way to control healthcare costs and allow real universal access is by addressing precisely these stakeholders, their inefficiency, and their profits.[47]

The Case for Medicare for All

The Political Consequences of Expanding Private Healthcare

The failure to achieve universal coverage through public provision did more than reflect the politics of healthcare in America; it also shaped these politics by fostering the growth of industries and groups profiting from the persistence of private healthcare finance. In Theodore Roosevelt's time, opposition came from doctors who profited from the system of private healthcare, as well as from those ideologically opposed to government intervention. By the time of FDR's administration, these had been joined by health insurance companies as well as some employers and unions who had established private plans. By the 1970s, pharmaceutical and medical device companies had joined the opposition, fearing that a public program would restrict their opportunities for profit. Over time, these interests have grown. Entire industries have now been created to profit from our private healthcare finance system, not only in the areas of medical devices, pharmaceuticals and health insurance, but also in relation to hospital networks, standalone imaging, laboratories, and urgent care clinics, the development of electronic medical record systems, bill processing and collection, and the financial analysis of health savings accounts. Private health insurance company revenues, already over 2% of national income in 1971, are 7% today. We have developed trillions of dollars' worth of vested interest in resisting a public healthcare finance system, with billions and billions being made in profits.

The Market Turn in Health Policy

If an omnipotent observer were to choose one program as a model for reforming American health-care, it would be Medicare. It has improved health for the elderly and reduced financial stress while controlling costs more effectively than does private health insurance.[48] For most of its history since 1970, Medicare has controlled per capita costs more effectively than have private insurers, with spending per enrollee rising 1.5 percentage points per year less from 1970 to 2016. Over that same period, while Medicare benefits have increased, notably with the prescription drug program, private insurance benefits have been cut by increasing deductibles and overall cost-sharing.[49]

Medicare's success has often been discounted, however, by policymakers and economists who have focused on its continued cost increases due to the rising and aging Medicare population, rather than on its success at containing price inflation. Paradoxically, Medicare has become more expensive because of population aging and longevity, which are marks of its success.[50] With some significant exceptions, economists distrust Medicare because it violates their bias towards "choice." Trained in orthodox neoclassical economics, with its ingrained faith in the efficiency of markets and market competition, many of the new health economists reject Medicare because it compels enrollment and then uses its market power to compel providers to accept a price list for services provided.

Ignoring Medicare's success, they have promoted choice in health insurance and in the provision of healthcare based on the idea that competition will encourage insurers and providers to become more efficient while giving "consumers" (otherwise known as the sick and disabled) the opportunity to choose the type and level of healthcare that they want as if they were choosing a brand of soda or a morning coffee. To make patients meaningful consumers, economists recommend reducing the insurance function, giving healthcare consumers "skin in the game" with higher cost-sharing, co-pays, and deductibles. Patient choice, they promise, will save money by discouraging overuse of health-

The Failure of Free Market Healthcare

care and encouraging insurers and providers to bring down the cost of care to increase their profit margins.[51]

By treating healthcare as a commodity and promoting choice, the market turn in healthcare policy rewards the young and healthy at the expense of the sick and the old. At the same time, introducing market mechanisms and profit immediately raises costs. Before the 1970s, health insurance was highly regulated, often with a single Blue Cross/Blue Shield plan offering simple coverage to everyone at a uniform price without regard for pre-existing conditions. Economists joined with insurance companies to campaign for deregulation to allow for-profit companies to compete with the Blue Cross/Blue Shield companies on the assumption that competition and the profit motive would lead to greater efficiency.

The economists were wrong. The new for-profit private insurance companies were no more efficient than the old Blue Cross/Blue Shield plans. But by restricting sales to the young and healthy, the new entrants made quick work of the established companies, who were quickly forced to abandon open enrollment policies and community rating. The mistake here was that policymakers misunderstood the real advantage that the new entrants

31

enjoyed. Far from increasing efficiency, administrative waste soared in for-profit companies, with increased spending on marketing, plan design, utilization review, managerial salaries, and, of course, profit. Rather than winning through efficiency, they profited by screening their subscribers. By offering plans attractive only to the healthiest, and cheapest, subscribers, they were able to make more money while driving the old Blues into bankruptcy with a pool of the sickest people.

Thus, the market turn drove up healthcare costs even while reducing Americans' access to care. As a result, we have a for-profit healthcare system that is more expensive than that of any other country while providing less care. But it generates profits and makes some people very rich. Which makes it very hard to change.

1

Why Markets *Cannot* Work in Healthcare

Professor Arrow's Classic

Awarded the Nobel Prize in Economics in 1972 at the age of 51, the youngest winner ever, Kenneth Arrow was an almost legendary figure in economics. A socialist in his youth, Arrow remained a social democrat throughout his life, but some of his most important work has often been misconstrued by conservatives as defending unregulated markets. Nowhere has this curious misconstruction been so powerful, and so pernicious, as in relation to Arrow's 1963 article, "Uncertainty and the Welfare Economics of Medical Care," which has since been cited nearly 10,000 times.[1]

Arrow's article was meant to bring the analysis of information to the study of imperfect competition.

Instead, it spawned a new field of health economics, where economists often cite Arrow before proceeding to discuss healthcare as if it is a commodity like cappuccinos or soft drinks. Few remember, if they ever understood, Arrow's point: medical care cannot be treated like other commodities because of fundamental information asymmetries. Alas, once they leave an author's pen, ideas take on a life of their own. If economists have used Arrow's words to make arguments contrary to his intent, all we can do is to try to recapture his meaning.

Arrow anticipated the failure of the market turn in healthcare. In well-functioning markets, competition among multiple suppliers drives costs and prices down to the cost of production because consumers seek out the highest quality at the lowest prices. This process does not work in healthcare due to information asymmetries that mean "consumers" (a.k.a. the sick and disabled) must rely on the judgment of others about what they need to buy, leading inevitably to concentrations of market power.[2]

The Problem of Healthcare Market Power

Healthcare will often be provided by institutions with market power. Providers operate in large facilities, like hospitals. Hospitals, specialist practices with dedicated machinery, pharmaceutical companies with large research facilities: all operate at a large scale that limits the number of competitors, giving each the power to influence prices.[3]

Even more important than scale, however, is the role of information. Few consumers can evaluate providers or treatment plans; even trained professionals do little better than amateurs in choosing providers.[4] Every doctor is different, patients with identical diagnoses are different, each doctor-patient relationship is different. Feeling unwell, patients go to a doctor, not knowing what problems they may face, or even if they have a problem. They enter physician offices largely unaware of the proper treatment they require. Instead of comparing essentially equivalent bars of soap, where buyers can evaluate price and quality, healthcare "consumers" compare providers of unknown and unknowable quality.

Facing such uncertainty, people rely on quality signals, brand names, reputation, the experience of others, advertising, even prices. Buying services that literally can be the difference between life and death, higher prices can increase demand because they are signals of quality. Signals steer patients to a small subset of providers who thus have real market power because people believe they provide better care and save lives. Massachusetts General Hospital, New York Presbyterian, Johns Hopkins, Yale New Haven, the Mayo Clinic, the Cleveland Clinic: these institutions do not compete on a level playing field with other hospitals and providers, and they advertise to further enhance their brands.[5] Their reputation gives them the leverage to raise prices.[6] The importance of reputation encourages providers to merge with marquee providers—hospitals with a reputation for extraordinary quality.

The Problem of Health Insurance

Arrow also highlighted the way uncertainty complicates the problem of health insurance. We do not know what healthcare we will need or when, or how much it will cost. Most of us, most of the time, spend little on healthcare; half of Americans spent less than $1000 in 2018. Or we may hit the jackpot: 1% spent nearly $200,000 in that same year. The only things that we know with certainty are that we will need healthcare, that it will be very expensive, and that having access to care may make the difference between our living and dying.

It is generally true that people prefer the security

of guaranteed small losses to the risk of very large ones. Since classical times, insurance has developed to provide that security by spreading the risk of very bad outcomes among larger groups. Facing the risk of fire, people buy homeowners insurance, paying a certain amount every year to receive money for a new home if needed. Facing mortality risk, people buy life insurance, accepting small losses in premiums for compensation in case of death. Facing the uncertainty of ill health and subsequent healthcare expense, people buy health insurance.

Arrow shows how asymmetric uncertainties create special problems for health insurance. Where no one knows the risks facing individuals, insurers can set premiums based on population averages, confident that the law of large numbers will generally protect them from extreme risk. But where subscribers have privileged information, insurers fear that anyone looking to buy insurance anticipates that they will need coverage. They fear "adverse selection," where people buy insurance because they know that they are more likely to need coverage than the population average, and so will cost more to cover than the insurance company expects. At the extreme is "moral hazard," where people buy insurance precisely because they intend to use the policy.[7]

Moral hazard and adverse selection lead to destructive insurance company practices, including the creation of an enormous wasteful bureaucracy dedicated to screening subscribers. Companies invest in bureaucrats, underwriters, claims adjusters and investigators, all to police subscribers and to screen for moral hazard and adverse selection. To discourage moral hazard and limit their risk from adverse selection, they limit the value of insurance with provisions for cost-sharing, deductibles, and co-pays, consciously reducing the social welfare gains from insurance. Insurers have also learned that they can profit by screening for certain subscribers. In a process called "cherry picking," they advertise for those unlikely to use insurance; by "lemon dropping," they discourage those more likely to need insurance. They have created giant research operations and marketing departments to develop better screening, including multiple plans with alternative benefit structures to steer potential subscribers towards plans more profitable to the insurer, at the expense of providing adequate coverage to the sick and needy.

Why Markets *Cannot* Work in Healthcare

Social Insurance and Health Insurance

While all insurance suffers from problems of uncertainty, adverse selection, and moral hazard, these problems are much greater for health insurance.[8] Life, homeowner or automobile insurers worry that people will destroy their own property, or even arrange their own deaths, to collect insurance. But these insurers usually find enough protection in a relatively small staff of insurance inspectors and, of course, the work of the police. In other cases, however, the risks of adverse selection and moral hazard are so severe that private insurance cannot function and insurance can only be provided by agencies with the legal authority to require universal coverage and to engage in more intrusive inspection to prevent fraud. For unemployment or income insurance, the risks of fraud are so great that private companies do not offer policies.[9] Public bodies offer coverage in these cases, through social insurance programs like Unemployment Insurance, because they can mandate universal coverage, eliminating the danger of adverse selection, and have the state authority to monitor behavior to reduce the danger of moral hazard.

As a society, we want people to receive quality healthcare because it raises productivity when people are healthy and because, as a community, we want people to live long, healthy lives. Most countries, then, treat health insurance like income insurance, with public provision to capture the benefits of insurance while avoiding adverse selection with universal provision and moral hazard through state supervision.

The case for social health insurance goes further, beyond efficiency to questions of equity, humanity, and citizenship. Valuing all as equal citizens, we do not want healthcare to be reserved only for those with the most money. Or, even worse, to trust healthcare decisions to private companies whose profits depend on their ability to deny access to healthcare. But this is exactly the situation with private health insurance. Insurers pay close attention to their "medical loss ratio" (MLR)—the share of insurance revenue paid out in health benefits— because a low ratio means that more is available for profits. Every dollar paid out in benefits is a dollar lost from profits.

For managers of insurance companies, a high MLR means they are suffering from adverse selection and moral hazard, but a low MLR shows that they are doing their job of maximizing profits. Insurance companies spend heavily to devise "cherry picking" programs to attract low-risk subscribers or to "lemon drop" in order to shed high-cost subscribers. Small-print advertisements, information sessions held in inaccessible locations, offers of gym memberships: all of these methods are used to sell insurance to healthy people while discouraging the elderly and less healthy. Successfully managing utilization, through cherry picking and lemon dropping, raises profits; failing to do so will lower profits and even risk bankruptcy.

The MLR thus measures more than company profits; it signals how well insurance companies undermine the benefits of insurance by denying it to the neediest. Here we see how use of the profit motive, which can work well in promoting the production of commodities, can promote inefficiency in healthcare. In their bid to raise profits, insurance companies waste resources though screening subscribers and establishing paperwork barriers to access. In doing so, they lower their MLR in ways that do not make us better off. These policies do nothing to enhance health. Insurance companies can increase their profits by driving away sick people, but the sick do not miraculously recover. Those unable to buy health insurance because they are at risk of illness and incurring high medical expenses disappear from an insurance company's pool of subscribers, but they remain part of the community—at least those among them who are not killed by insurance company toxicity.

The Market Turn in Health Policy: Motivation and Rationales

Although some economists have criticized the behavior of private insurance companies, many regularly provide rationalizations for their actions, even claiming they are socially useful. Viewing all problems through the prism of perfect commodity markets, many economists have come to believe that health insurance promotes unnecessary utilization because insured "consumers" do not pay the full cost of their care. They claim that people receiving healthcare at a cost below the marginal cost of providing that care will only abuse the system, much as they would eat too many donuts if they were free. Ignoring all the other costs of receiving healthcare, and all the ways insurance companies restrict utilization, they argue that the problem of high healthcare spending occurs because healthcare consumers are profligate when spending someone else's money.[10]

This focus on overutilization has created an alliance between the health insurance industry and the economists behind programs to restrict access. Economists have favored opening up health insurance markets to competition because they claim only for-profit private companies can be trusted to restrain "overutilization" and "abuse." Yet, even the effective collapse of not-for-profit health insurers in the 1980s failed to restrain the rapid growth in healthcare spending. Instead, moneys saved from reducing utilization were spent on growing bureaucratic waste, even while economists helped insurance companies to develop elaborate tools to restrict utilization, including cost-sharing, deductibles, and co-pays, and changes in payment systems to discourage providers from caring for the sick. Still, many economists have continued to support spending by insurers to police the use of healthcare, including utilization reviews and requirements for preauthorization for care.[11]

The new world of healthcare finance created by this alliance of economists and insurance companies has done many things, but it has not controlled spending. It has created mountains of paper and wasteful administration devoted to policing providers and patients, driving many nurses and physicians to distraction, even to early retirement. It has reduced the insurance function by providing less protection for the sick and needy, undermining the quality of care Americans receive. In short, the market turn has brought us to this worst of all possible worlds: an overpriced healthcare system that does not provide adequate healthcare.

Wasteful administration comes both in the administration of insurance companies and in bill processing within provider offices, hospitals and physician practices. First, there is the cost of administering insurance companies, including their profits but also the money they spend cherry picking and lemon dropping, and restraining moral hazard by discouraging utilization. Private health insurance is an expensive way to provide coverage. Insurers have managed to drive down the medical loss ratio to under 80%, meaning that over 20 cents of every dollar paid in premiums goes towards administrative costs, including marketing, profit, management salaries, and utilization reviews.[12] In 2018, the United States spent over $256 billion on administration of the private health insurance system, an expense expected to pass $400 billion by 2026. By contrast, traditional public social insurance, Medicare, spends over 98 cents of every dollar providing care.[13] Compared with Medicare, the extra cost of providing coverage through private companies amounted to over $200 billion in 2018, and the tab has kept rising.

Why Markets *Cannot* Work in Healthcare

Clearly, competition has not driven health insurance companies to minimize costs. The mistake economists have made—one that they make again and again in relation to the healthcare system—is to believe that the search for profit will lead companies to provide quality healthcare at affordable prices. For private health insurers, administrative waste is efficient if it reduces medical losses, either by discouraging utilization, allowing the company to avoid making payments, or by controlling selection among subscribers. While money spent on administration and reviewing claims is a social waste that does nothing to provide better care, it is profitable for insurers if it leads to lemon dropping and cherry picking, or if it discourages utilization. Research that leads to carefully targeted advertising, programs that make policies more attractive to young, healthy people and less attractive to older, sicker people: these can save money way beyond any increase in administrative expense. And in doing so they raise profits.

Of course, for our community, such policies are pure waste, and worse. Depriving the sick of health insurance makes us sicker, even to the point of killing us.

The Cost of Using the Market to Provide Healthcare

The $200 billion administrative burden within health insurance companies only scratches the surface of the cost of the market turn in healthcare policy. Employers spend around $50 billion (4% of employer-provided health insurance) a year on consultants and brokers who help them to identify and negotiate health insurance for their workers. And this does not include the costs to HR departments of processing paper for the insurance industry, nor the cost to individual subscribers in completing forms and submitting claims.[14] Insurers have succeeded in offloading even more of their administrative waste by imposing expensive, even onerous, reporting requirements on providers and those seeking healthcare. American healthcare providers (hospitals, physicians, etc.) spend significantly more time on administrative tasks than do their counterparts in countries with universal coverage systems.[15] Our physicians, for example, devote over six hours a week to administrative tasks, notably bill processing, four times as much as their counterparts in Canada, where hospitals and physician practices can manage with minimal billing departments because all their billing goes to one government agency.[16] American hospitals and physicians require nearly eight times as many staff to process bills as in other industries.[17] Even other countries that rely on private health insurance, like Switzerland or the Netherlands, have a lower administrative burden for providers through regulations that standardize benefit packages and payment systems.

Compared with Canada's single-payer system, on top of the $200 billion we spend within insurance companies on excess administration, we spend nearly $200 billion more on administration within provider offices. This brings the extra administrative burden of the market turn and the reliance on private for-profit health insurance to $400 billion—almost twice as much as we spend on nursing and home healthcare.

Do we get anything for this $400 billion? We certainly do not get controls over provider prices. Economists expected that competing insurance companies would negotiate to bring down the inflated prices charged by drug companies, hospitals, or other providers, but, again, they misunderstood the healthcare marketplace. Medicare is the only system with the market power to secure lower prices. The large number of competing private insurers are too small to have the market leverage to negotiate effectively with providers.

Elite hospitals and drug and medical device manufacturers have made short shrift of insurance companies. During the debate over the Affordable Care Act, for example, insurance industry lobbyists—notably Karen Ignagni of America's Health Insurance Plans (AHIP)—supported many of the Obama administration's initiatives in alliance with economists who sought to strengthen insurance companies against hospitals and drug companies.[18] Alas, insurance companies have been weak reeds, unable to protect the public from predacious providers with market power. The problem, as Arrow would have predicted, is that there are many insurance companies, but only one Massachusetts General Hospital or one Cleveland Clinic; many insurance companies, but only one company that makes Sovaldi (for Hepatitis C) or Folotyn (for T-Cell Lymphoma). When it comes to bargaining, the fallback position for the two sides is profoundly unbalanced. Insurers risk losing subscribers if they cannot provide access to life-saving medications or elite hospitals, but those hospitals or drug companies can easily absorb the loss of business from any individual insurer. The one exception, Medicare, proves the rule: it alone is large enough to ensure that hospitals cannot afford to lose its business, even at a dramatically lower pay scale.

Why Markets *Cannot* Work in Healthcare

It gets worse. Not only does the fragmented private insurance industry fail to restrain price abuses by big hospitals and Big Pharma, but when insurers try to restrain prices, they do so in ways that necessarily undermine the quality of our healthcare. Effective bargaining depends on the ability to walk away if the price is not right. Health insurers only "walk away" by restricting access to high-priced providers, barricading members within narrow networks. This creates health problems as many people are regularly forced to change providers or drug regimens when their insurer renegotiates provider contracts. For those with the same insurance plan, this can happen regularly when plans renegotiate their provider networks. And it happens every time people change insurance plans, either because their employer chooses a different plan or because they change jobs. A recent survey for Michigan found that after one year 72% of those with employer-sponsored health insurance had a different plan, either because they switched jobs or changed to a different employer-sponsored plan.[19] Every change risks moving to a new insurance network that will compel a change of physician or drugs, with further possible risks to health.[20]

For all the damage to health, the efforts of private health insurance have failed to restrain soaring prices for US hospital services, medical devices, and drugs, prices far higher than are paid anywhere else.[21] We pay twice as much for drugs as the rest of the world and much higher prices for hospital services.[22] While Medicare has continued to control hospital prices effectively, mergers have created consolidated hospital networks so powerful that the Congressional Budget Office estimates private health insurance now pays rates nearly twice as high as Medicare.[23] Hospitals have also been buying up physician practices so that a large majority of American primary care physicians are now employed by larger bodies able to charge higher prices.[24] Market power is allowing providers to drive prices higher at the expense of the general public.[25]

Inflated prices for drugs and medical devices cost Americans over $200 billion, while hospitals charge private payers as much as $400 billion more than Medicare rates. Add to this $600 billion the $400 billion in administrative waste in provider offices and insurance companies and we pay over $1 trillion more for healthcare (see Figure 5, below p. 62). Each American is paying over $3000 in extra healthcare costs to maintain our system of for-profit, market-driven medicine.

This is a steep price to pay for the inappropriate application of economic reasoning to healthcare.

2

Can We Afford
Medicare for All?

*"It Costs Too Much, and Would
Destroy Everything"*

Critics of Medicare have had their say. Drawing on
a study by the libertarian Mercatus Center, *Time
Magazine* warns that Medicare for All "would
boost government health spending by $32.6 trillion
over 10 years" and require historic tax hikes, more
than doubling current federal income tax collec-
tions. Just to underline the point, *Time* adds "that's
trillion with a 'T.'"[1] Seema Verma, head of the
Centers for Medicare and Medicaid Services, warns
of a $2.5 trillion tax hike to fund Medicare for
All.[2] She exaggerates. The Mercatus study she cites
puts the tax hike at under $2 trillion and acknowl-
edges that this is less than the money saved from

dispensing with private health insurance premiums and reducing out-of-pocket spending projected under the current system. In any case, attacks on Medicare for All rely on fear, not arithmetic, good or bad. Medicare for All would apparently entail a "government takeover." "Government-run" healthcare would eviscerate "the private insurance marketplace," destroying employer-provided health insurance, and even the current Medicare system.[3] It would undermine the entire economy, "eviscerating [that word again] the stock, bond and commercial real estate markets."[4] Salaries and opportunities in healthcare would be reduced, destroying our system of medical education and our university system. Research and development and the discovery of new drugs and medical treatments would stop. Healthcare throughout the world would suffer because profits earned in the United States power healthcare innovation everywhere.[5]

Wow. That sure sounds horrible. But is anything in this critique even remotely true?

The critics miss the point. First, Medicare for All would do nothing to change the *provision* of healthcare; it is only concerned with the *financing*. The provision of care, the way people fill prescriptions or receive care from doctors and hospitals, would not change at all. Why would it? Already nearly half of healthcare is financed by the government without disrupting relationships between patients and caregivers. In existing Medicare, people choose a physician and see them as needed, physicians treat patients as they believe appropriate, and Medicare is billed at established rates. Medicare for All would change nothing because it would continue to operate under the same insurance model as existing Medicare. Everyone would choose doctors just as the elderly and disabled do under Medicare now. Doctors and hospitals would treat patients according to their medical needs and would be paid according to a price list set as under Medicare now. People would fill prescriptions and buy medical devices paid for by Medicare, as happens now.

The only change for people currently receiving Medicare is that Medicare for All would provide comprehensive benefits without cost-sharing, eliminating the need for any private Medigap coverage. And it would be tax-funded, eliminating the premiums now paid for Part B (physician services).

While leaving the doctor–patient relationship unchanged, Medicare for All would address the three great problems afflicting the current system: declining coverage, waning access, and rising costs. No one would go without insurance because everyone would be covered automatically without regard for any pre-existing medical conditions. Medicare for All would end the distinction between in network/out of network and give everyone a full choice of physician. It would end insurance denial of coverage and requirements for prior authorization, restoring physicians' discretion to treat patients and prescribe drugs or devices according to their medical judgment. Costs would be controlled with savings from simplified billing processes, administration, and negotiated pricing. These are changes that would benefit all Americans.

Nonetheless, beyond the right-wing hyperbole, the critique of Medicare for All does raise legitimate issues that advocates really do need to address:

- *Is it too big a change?*
- *Is it a government takeover of healthcare?*
- *Will there be interminable wait times for care?*
- *Will we lose the initiative for productive innovation?*
- *Is it a nice idea that costs too much?*

Is it too big a change?

Medicare for All would not change the practice of medicine. It would liberate physicians and patients from the oversight of insurance companies and others who profit from restricting our access to healthcare. Changes would be on the financing side. Instead of doctors and hospitals billing multiple insurance companies, they will bill only one.[6] Instead of negotiating each bill and navigating a system of co-pays, deductibles, prior approvals, and utilization reviews, payments will be made by a single agency with rules and prices set to protect health not insurance company profits. The time that doctors and nurses now spend pushing paper for health insurers would be available for patient care.[7]

Nothing in Medicare for All entails a change in the way healthcare is delivered by nurses and physicians. For patients, the difference is that they would no longer be restricted in their choice of provider or procedure, and would no longer have to worry about whether a doctor is 'in network' or a procedure or recommended drug is approved by the insurance company.[8]

A government takeover?

Clearly, this is not a government takeover of healthcare. Medicare for All is not the British National Health Service or the Veterans Administration, where doctors and nurses are directly employed by the government. Some favor such an approach, but it is not what is done in Medicare in the United States, nor in Canada or Taiwan or other countries with similar systems, nor is it what is proposed in the Medicare for All legislation in Congress. Healthcare will continue to be provided by private entities. Doctors and many hospitals will continue to operate as private bodies. They will be regulated by government as they are now, but they will continue to be managed independently. Perhaps most important, those unhappy with their government-financed healthcare will still be free to seek alternatives from doctors and hospitals who would remain free to serve anyone.

With Medicare for All, government will continue to regulate healthcare and approve procedures and drugs as it does now. The change will be in the financing of a comprehensive insurance policy available to everyone. With such a policy in place, the actual administration of the insurance program need not be done by civil servants employed by the government. Bill processing, fraud prevention, and utilization review—indeed all aspects of insurance administration—can be done by private agencies, as in the current Medicare system.

Long wait times for care?

Eliminating cost-sharing and extending insurance to the uninsured will raise demand for services but the healthcare system will be able to handle this without extended wait times because reducing administrative waste will free up enough physician and nurse time to accommodate the increased demand. Critics misunderstand this because they mistakenly assume the system is efficient now, but in arguing that Medicare for All would dramatically increase utilization, they implicitly acknowledge that the current system rations access because so many Americans cannot afford to seek care.[9] Indeed, wait times are not generally longer for public systems providing universal coverage.[10] Where wait times are significantly longer, it is because countries choose to focus spending on what they see as higher value care. Like most countries, Canada, for example, has fewer MRI machines per capita than the US, but many more primary care doctors, allowing Canadians to see physicians almost twice as frequently as do people in the United States.[11]

Compared to Canada and other countries, the US has much more rationing of healthcare and longer wait times because of unaffordable costs and the lack of access to adequate insurance. More important than wait times for a few elective specialist services is the very large difference in the proportion of the sick who even try to see a doctor. Only 6% of Canadians report that in the last year they "had a medical problem but did not visit a doctor because of cost." The proportion in the United States that did not visit a doctor because of cost is four times as large.[12]

Won't taking out the profits kill innovation?

If we remove the profit motive from healthcare, will doctors and researchers stop discovering new drugs and better ways to treat disease? Superficially, this may appear to be a serious concern. The United States has been the source of many of the new technologies in modern medicine, from the mass availability of antibiotics through to vaccines for polio, and Americans have played a major role in the development of MRI machines and other medical devices. Yet none of these developments came as a response to opportunities to profit. The technology of mass production of penicillin was developed by the US military during World War II. Jonas Salk discovered his polio vaccine in the United States, but, like Frederick Banting with insulin, he donated it to the world. Many have profited from MRI, but not its inventors, Paul Lauterbur and Peter Mansfield, who remained active professors throughout their lives, with Lauterbur's original research being conducted while serving in the US Army. There are many reasons to seek to develop new medical technologies: intellectual adventure, a desire to save lives and do good, winning the respect of one's colleagues and neighbors. All of these, rather than profit, drove Banting, Salk, Lauterbur, Mansfield, and others.

Most productive pharmaceutical research is not funded by US companies. In Europe, as well as in the United States, major developments depend on public sector funding. The long lead time on truly innovative research and the great risk of failure are powerful deterrents to any private investment, which is why virtually all of the major innovations in drug therapies and other medical areas have been publicly financed.[13]

Extraordinarily high profits for drug companies are not necessary for research and innovation in healthcare, nor have they provided particularly strong incentives for constructive work. In theory, the profit motive may encourage valuable innovations, but it has also led to waste and destruction. The greater margin on drug sales in the United States produces profits twice as high as the total research and development spending by American drug companies; lowering prices to a level where the surplus would cover all pharmaceutical research would have saved Americans over $40 billion in 2015, 12% of all US drug spending that year.[14] US drug companies claim to spend over $70 billion on research and development, but nearly half of this is done using public funds provided through tax credits and other subsidies.[15] Added to this $30 billion in subsidies to drug companies is the almost $40 billion in direct government spending for medical research through the National Institutes of Health. When research funded by the Veterans Administration and other government agencies is included, as well as charitable research funding from various foundations, total public medical research spending is easily twice that of the private sector. Discounting private sector research on packaging, naming, and marketing, the great majority of serious research is publicly financed.[16]

Profit-seeking by pharmaceutical companies does not necessarily benefit the public. The search for profit led Purdue Pharma to invest millions in formulating and executing marketing strategies for its OxyContin drug, leading to huge profits for the company where the rate of return far exceeded that from any legitimate research.[17] While most private sector research is less toxic, much is of little social value. Private companies shun long-term investments in basic research to focus on marketing or, even worse, on "evergreening"—making slight modifications in drugs to extend patents and prevent the sale of generic versions. "Typically," in the words of Dr. Joel Lexchin, "when you evergreen something, you are not looking at any significant therapeutic advantage. You are looking at a company's economic advantage."[18] From 2005 to 2015, 74% of the new drug patents in FDA records were awarded to existing drugs, not new medications. In that period, almost 80% of the 100 best-selling pharmaceutical products were awarded an add-on patent or other type of exclusivity extension, nearly half of them more than once.[19]

While profitable, such research and development work does nothing to enhance health. Worse, by diverting scarce intellectual resources and promoting patent litigation, it retards innovation even while the exorbitant prices charged for these drugs deny millions of Americans access to them. Taking account of the negative effects of most of their R&D, it is not clear whether the $40 billion of their own money that pharmaceutical companies claim to invest yields any net positive social benefit.

Nice idea, but how can we afford it?
We can afford a better healthcare system because Medicare for All will allow savings through simplified billing, savings on the administration of insurance, and savings from lowering the prices paid to monopolistic pharmaceutical companies

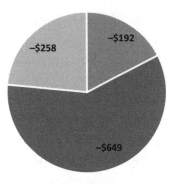

Provider administration ■ Reduction to Medicare negotiated rates ■ Insurance administration

Figure 5: Medicare for All savings, 2019, compared with current system

Note: This figure shows projected savings, in billions, from instituting a program of Medicare for All in 2019 for three areas of healthcare spending: provider administration, insurance administration, and payments to hospitals, medical equipment manufacturers, and drug companies.

and hospitals (see Figure 5). Over time, the savings will increase because Medicare for All will slow the rate of healthcare price inflation (see Figure 6).

The bottom line is, if we can afford the current system with all its waste and inefficiencies, we can afford a simpler, more efficient system: Medicare for All.

Eliminating the private insurance system would have saved $245 billion in 2019 (see Figure 5). To this needs to be added the nearly $200 billion in savings from provider administration, because under Medicare for All hospitals and physician practices will no longer need so many bill collectors. An uncounted benefit: nurses and doctors will be able to spend time providing patient care instead of negotiating with insurance companies, and Americans will live longer and healthier lives.

Unlike private insurance companies, Medicare already has the market power to negotiate realistic prices with hospitals, equipment manufacturers, and pharmaceutical companies. Instead of prices set by providers with market power, prices will be negotiated by a Medicare for All system with the market power that stems from its position of being responsible for paying for the healthcare of Americans. It can then negotiate prices in line with the real costs of providing healthcare, prices more in keeping with those paid by people outside the United States. Adopting world prices for drugs and medical devices would have saved the US over $200 billion in 2019. Eliminating the surcharge above Medicare prices collected by hospitals and drug companies would have saved another $400 billion.

Putting it all together, Medicare for All could have saved over $1 trillion in 2019, bringing per-capita healthcare spending down to the level of other affluent countries. Over ten years, the gross

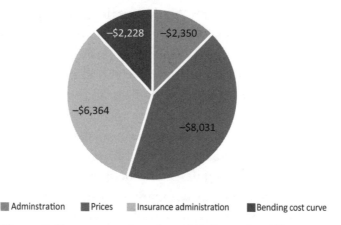

Administration **Prices** Insurance administration **Bending cost curve**

Figure 6: Ten-year savings from Medicare for All

Note: This figure shows projected savings over ten years, in billions, from instituting a program of Medicare for All in 2019 for three areas of healthcare spending: provider administration, insurance administration, and payments to hospitals, medical equipment manufacturers, and drug companies. In addition, savings are shown to be achieved by "bending the cost curve," or slowing the rate of growth in healthcare spending by 1.1%, to a rate comparable to that in Canada.

savings would come to nearly $20 trillion (see Figure 6).

There are additional costs associated with a program of universal coverage (see Figure 7), but these should be balanced against the significant health benefits they would produce. First, there is the cost of covering the uninsured, currently about 9% of the population. Giving them full access to healthcare would save some money by allow-

Can We Afford Medicare for All?

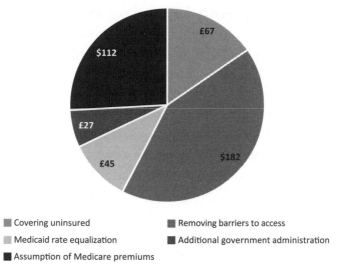

Covering uninsured
Medicaid rate equalization
Assumption of Medicare premiums
Removing barriers to access
Additional government administration

Figure 7: Medicare for All additional costs, 2019, compared with current system

Note: This figure shows the additional costs, in billions, from instituting a program of Medicare for All in 2019 for five areas of healthcare spending: covering the uninsured, removing cost-sharing and other financial barriers to access, raising Medicaid rates to the level of other reimbursements, eliminating Medicare Part B premiums, and the cost of administering the program.

ing for more preventive measures and by shifting some healthcare from hospital emergency rooms to regular physician practices. Also, the uninsured are a relatively inexpensive group to cover because they are younger than those with insurance. Because of Medicare, the current insured population already includes the elderly and disabled. Taking account of the savings, covering the uninsured would add over $60 billion to our healthcare spending.

Removing co-pays, deductibles, and barriers to access is a policy decision not necessary for a Medicare for All program.[20] Any reduction in these barriers will lead to increases in the utilization of healthcare. However, historical experience shows that these increases may not be as great as might be found for other products, like shoes or birdfeeders. In some cases, eliminating cost-sharing has had surprisingly little impact on health spending. In Canada and Taiwan, for example, there was little increase in spending when these countries moved to single-payer systems.[21] This may be because most medical expenses were outside of individual control due to major illness or accident and were directed by medical providers.[22] In addition, we need to be aware of the benefits from increased utilization; while cost-sharing and lack of insurance deter people from seeking medical care, removing these may lead to greater use of preventive care, thereby lowering costs in the long run.

By providing preventive care and allowing providers to identify illnesses early, before they become more severe, it may be the case that removing cost-sharing would have little effect on costs, especially over time. To be conservative, however, I have made a relatively large estimate of the effect of removing cost-sharing.[23] Using figures from the Centers for Medicare and Medicaid Statistics of the effect of cost-sharing on utilization, I project that utilization would increase by 7.4% with the elimination of cost-sharing at a cost of nearly $200 billion.[24]

There are other costs that are redistributive, rather than representing actual increases in the cost of providing healthcare. Under a single-payer system, for example, Medicaid providers would be paid at the same price as other providers, at an added cost of $45 billion. (This should also help to provide better access to medical services for Medicaid recipients, and equity to their providers.) An even larger benefit would go to the elderly who would no longer be burdened with premiums for Medicare, at a cost of $112 billion; this increases the cost of the program while providing equivalent, dollar for dollar savings for the elderly and disabled. The elderly would also benefit from the elimination of Medicare co-pays, deductibles, and the cost of Medicare wraparound policies.[25]

Whatever the costs of universal coverage and increased utilization, they need to be balanced against the benefits of improved population health. If the current system increases annual mortality by 300,000 (see Figure 3), incurring extra costs of $2.7

trillion, then that saving should be balanced against any increase in cost from Medicare for All.

Even on a narrow cash basis, Medicare for All would have lowered healthcare spending in 2019 by well over $500 billion, a saving achieved by eliminating the waste inherent in private insurance and the overpricing of goods and services by providers with market power. A public system of universal coverage could thus provide healthcare more efficiently, and at a lower cost, than a private market system. The question of whether we can afford Medicare for All should therefore be reframed: the real question is how much longer we can afford the current system.

Paying for Medicare for All

Moving to Medicare for All will involve dramatic reductions in current spending for health insurance premiums and out-of-pocket healthcare, balanced by net savings and increased taxes. As critics have noted, over the ten years 2019 to 2028, Medicare for All would cost nearly $36 trillion, which would require an increase in federal revenues of nearly $9 trillion over the same period.[26]

This tax increase, however, would be more than offset for Americans by the reduction in health

Can We Afford Medicare for All?

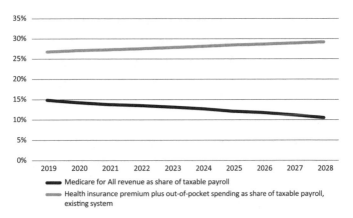

Figure 8: Medicare for All savings as share of taxable payroll

Note: This figure shows the projected cost of the current private health insurance system and out-of-pocket spending compared with the cost of Medicare for All as a share of taxable payroll, under the assumption that all of the Medicare for All revenue would be collected from wages and salaries.

insurance premiums and out-of-pocket spending on healthcare.[27] Current insurance premiums are already nearly 22% of taxable payroll and are projected to rise to nearly 24% over the next decade, well above the cost of Medicare for All at 14% of taxable payroll, falling to 10% over the next decade (see Figure 8). If the total cost of the Medicare for All system was put on wages, it would still lower the share of wages going to healthcare by a third, saving the average worker over $4000 in 2019, rising to nearly $8000 by 2028 (see Figure 8). The savings for the average worker would be even greater to the extent that Medicare for All is financed with progressive taxation, which would shift some of the cost onto those with more ability to pay, and onto profits. Health insurance premiums currently are the same for all regardless of income: a CEO who is paid $20 million pays the same premium as a sales agent on $50,000. By shifting the burden to ability to pay, tax finance would give even greater savings to the middle class and to workers.

The Real Economic Issue

If we can afford the current system, then we can afford something cheaper. If we can tolerate the current system with all its inequities and inefficiencies, causing the deaths of literally tens of thousands of Americans each year, then we could tolerate a system that would provide better healthcare to all Americans. If our businesses and our workers can pay for a system that fixes the burden on them, limiting their ability to compete in the world economy, then they could bear a system that reduces the burden on everyone and spreads it across all forms of income. If our doctors and nurses and other healthcare professionals can navigate the current Byzantine system, then they could manage one that simplifies their work and allows them to focus on providing better healthcare to all Americans.

In short, Medicare for All is so superior to the current system on all accounts that the only question is why we haven't introduced it yet.

3

From Here to There Is Politics

Why Is It So Hard?

We have built a healthcare system with over $3 trillion of vested interests; as a result, many of the richest and most powerful Americans have much to lose from any change of system. These losses would be both substantial and definite compared with the prospective benefits that most of us would enjoy from Medicare for All. Every dollar that we anticipate saving by fixing the broken healthcare finance system is part of someone's income, and because so much of that income is concentrated in the high salaries and profits enjoyed by some of the richest Americans, the fight for Medicare for All involves a titanic political challenge.

Even the current system's worst failings inhibit

change. The anxiety it creates incites in people the fear of losing what little security they still have. This leads many to hold tight to their current insurance. We can promise a better system, but what people know for sure is that they will be losing what they have now. Healthy skepticism about Medicare for All is quite rational.[1] We can tell people all about the benefits of Medicare for All, but these are prospective benefits, discounted by a reasonable sense that they may or may not actually happen: things may work as well as we anticipate but they may not, and when it comes to something as important as healthcare, people seek security. On the other side, those who benefit from the current system believe with certainty that Medicare for All would threaten their inflated profits. And everyone knows that taxes will rise.

The interests at stake

Opponents of Medicare capitalize on what one former insurance executive, Wendell Potter, calls FUD, "Fear, Uncertainty, Doubt," and will spend vast sums to spread it.[2] We might expect nothing less because they have so much money at stake. Under Medicare for All, we can spend less while providing more services because we will be reducing administrative bloat and the profits and inflated managerial salaries that it protects. In 2017, the nine largest health insurance companies in the country had a market value of just under $400 billion, representing the present value of the future profits that investors expect to make off all of us. In the same year, their CEOs had an average pay of $15 million (see Table 2), nearly 100 times the salary of the head of the federal government's Centers for Medicare and Medicaid Services, a woman responsible for the healthcare of nearly half of all Americans. While health insurance company executives are paid the most, there are others who also live well off our healthcare system. CEOs of the largest insurance companies, hospitals, and pharmaceutical companies took home $540 million in compensation, an average of over $10 million apiece. Only two hospital executives were paid under $2 million.

Every drug company manager, hospital director, and insurance company CEO understands what Medicare for All would mean for their companies and their own paychecks. Members of the economic elite beyond these companies also have interests in the current privatized healthcare system. Around every healthcare enterprise there orbits a plethora of economic interests. Directors of banks, mutual funds, and pension programs

Table 2: Market value, debt, CEO pay, and employees of the nine largest health insurance companies, around 2016–17

Company	Market Value (in millions) (9/20/2017)	Long-Term Debt (2016) (in millions)	CEO Total Compensation (2016 Fiscal Year)	Employees
UnitedHealth Group	$189,263	$25,777	$15,695,513	230,000
Anthem	$48,181	$14,359	$16,455,697	53,000
Aetna	$51,485	$19,027	$18,653,231	49,500
Cigna	$45,779	$4756	$15,217,857	41,000
Humana	$34,639	$4279	$19,722,400	51,600
Centene Corporation	$15,654	$4651	$21,968,983	30,500
WellCare Health Plans	$7374	$998	$9,260,080	7400
Molina Healthcare	$3575	$773	$9,883,419	21,000
Magellan Health	$1918	$238	$7,451,383	9700

Note: This table shows the financial interests in the nine largest health insurance companies, including their stock market value, long-term debt, CEO compensation, and number of employees as of 2016.

75

Table 3: CEO compensation, major health insurers, 2016
fiscal year

Insurer	CEO	CEO Total Compensation
UnitedHealth Group	Stephen J. Hemsley	$15,695,513
Anthem	Joseph R. Swedish	$16,455,697
Aetna	Mark T. Bertolini	$18,653,231
Cigna	David Michael Cordani	$15,217,857
Humana	Bruce D. Broussard	$19,722,400
Centene Corporation	Michael F. Neidorff	$21,968,983
Health Net	Jay M. Gellert	$11,897,512
WellCare Health Plans	Ken Burdick	$9,260,080
Molina Healthcare	J. Mario Molina	$9,883,419
Magellan Health	Barry M. Smith	$7,451,383

Sources: Company reports

manage the funds of such enterprises, and often
have equity shares in them. Real estate companies
and other local economic interests benefit from
proximity to successful hospitals. Investors hold
over $75 billion in bonds and other long-term debt
issued by healthcare companies. Add to these the
banks who profit from processing their payment
systems—a cash flow of hundreds of billions of
dollars—the independent brokers and consultants
who profit from the sale of insurance products,
and the media companies, marketing agents, and
advertising firms who profit from their marketing
budgets. Even the economists who help design their

plans and coordinate their cash flows have an interest in stopping Medicare for All.

The Harry and Louise advertising campaign from the early 1990s is a good example of how the health insurance industry defends itself. Costing $20 million, the campaign not only helped beat back the Clinton health reform program but also bought the insurance industry allies in the public relations and entertainment industries. Health industry firms also benefit from our peculiar national policy of allowing the advertising of pharmaceuticals. Healthcare advertising spending rose to almost $10 billion in 2015, almost 60% of which came from pharmaceutical companies and another 23% from hospitals.[3] Madison Avenue, of course, profits from this, as do the television networks and other media companies. Celebrities get their piece. There is a long list from A to Z of celebrities paid to speak for drug companies.[4] Jennifer Aniston appears in an "educational campaign" from Shire, the maker of Xiidra dry-eye medication.[5] Bon Jovi promotes Advil, Brooke Shields hawks Latisse, Rob Lowe sells Amgen, and, of course, Bob Dole speaks up for erectile dysfunction (courtesy of Pfizer).

With so much money at stake it should be no surprise that insurance companies, hospitals, and pharmaceutical companies spend more on lobbying

Washington than does any other industry.[6] Their representatives swarm Capitol Hill and the 50 state capitals, advising lawmakers, drafting legislation, and attending campaign fundraising events. Health industry groups carefully spread their money among both political parties to maintain access regardless of who wins elections.[7] Pharmaceutical companies spent $216 million on lobbying activities in 2018, the most of any industrial sector. Other healthcare companies are also among the most active lobbyists, including insurance, second at $121 million, and hospitals and nursing homes at $74 million. Wall Street and the vaunted military-industrial complex cannot compare to the lobbying clout deployed by the health industrial complex.

Lobbies do more than directly influence government, and their most pernicious effect may be to distort public dialogue. Many businesses fund academic research, usually with a strong bias towards research directed at supporting their own programs. The role of pharmaceutical companies in promoting research on therapies they can profitably commercialize is well documented.[8] Just as important is the way healthcare companies shape social science research to narrow the range of politically viable ideas. The role of openly right-wing foundations is well known, but others also use money to buy research.[9] Johnson & Johnson, for example, sponsors one of the most active foundations in healthcare, the Robert Wood Johnson Foundation, and the family that created Kaiser Permanente similarly sponsors the Kaiser Family Foundation. The boards of directors of both foundations are carefully structured to stake out an acceptable range of policy options, favoring incremental changes while preserving our private health insurance system. Kaiser's board, for example, spans the spectrum from Dr. William Frist (of the Hospital Corporation of America) on the right, through the centrist former Republican senator from Maine, Olympia Snowe, to, on the left, prominent supporters of the Affordable Care Act.[10] Missing are advocates of national health insurance, academics critical of for-profit medicine, and representatives of organized labor or patient advocacy groups.

The health industry funds social science research to promote incremental changes with short-term policy relevance. In practice, this means introducing measures that extend the existing system of health insurance to more people while shifting the burden of rising costs onto individuals who use healthcare.[11] This leads to a deep research agenda focused on the elasticity of demand for healthcare and the effect of moral hazard on healthcare expenditures.

While such research is well funded, less is spent on understanding the administrative waste or over-charging in the current system.[12] Ten recent research grants from the Robert Wood Johnson foundation, for example, include six programs under the broad rubric of "culture of health," directed at measuring the cost of individual behaviors and devising strate-gies to teach individuals to behave differently. No research grants, however, address the health effects of restrictive insurance networks or cost-sharing. (While regularly warning of the dangers of stress, none of these programs address the stress produced by restrictive insurance networks or cost-sharing!) Nor do any grants in this round address the admin-istrative burden of the current healthcare system or the excessive profits earned by drug companies and consolidated hospital networks.[13] Focusing on the individual determinants of health, such as diet or the consumption of alcohol, provides a distraction from investigating the social determinants of health, including the financing of our healthcare system.

To Cross a Chasm, Build Bridges

The campaign for Medicare for All needs a massive social movement to elect politicians committed to universal healthcare and to hold them accountable for delivering it. But it needs much more than this. To win, we need to reassure the public that our program is viable, both by demonstrating real success in the form of palpable accomplishments and by establishing tangible state capacity. Right now, we don't have the votes, so we need to seek allies who will help transform the environment to win more public support and move in the direction of Medicare for All. These allies will include advocates of incremental reforms: allies who may only walk part of the way with us but can help to accomplish the intermediate goals that will pave the way for larger reforms.

In short, we need a smart politics. What I propose are measures that will bring us closer to Medicare for All by transforming the political environment along three dimensions: demonstrating viability, building state capacity, and disarming opposition. By working on these three dimensions, the proposed incremental measures are suggested as steps towards the goal, Medicare For All. They are not substitutes for Medicare For All. They are way stations. The end goal remains universal coverage through a public agency, Medicare For All.

Demonstrate viability by showing that government can save money: Negotiate drug prices

Americans with private insurance or Medicare pay twice as much for drugs as do people in other countries, and twice what the Veterans Administration pays. We can extend the VA's success in negotiating lower drug prices through Medicare for All, even strengthening the government's bargaining hand by threatening to eliminate patent protection or to buy patents under eminent domain. Measures to restrict the pricing of pharmaceuticals can help in building alliances with employers paying for health insurance, state governments, hospitals, and even health insurers.[14]

Demonstrate viability by showing that government can lower prices: Antitrust action against companies that use market power to inflate prices

The highest rates of medical inflation over the past decades have been in the sectors with the highest rates of provider consolidation: hospitals and pharmaceuticals. There are potential allies here, including employers and state governments, who would benefit from bringing down inflated hospital and pharmaceutical prices.

Demonstrate viability and build capacity:
Mandate simplified and uniform coverage and
protect those with pre-existing conditions

By extending the insurance regulations in the Affordable Care Act—to mandate common policies for all insurers and to maintain protections for those with pre-existing conditions—we would win allies among employers and others who pay for healthcare by simplifying competition and choice and lowering prices. Squeezing some of the administrative waste out of the insurance system would ease the transition to Medicare for All by establishing uniform coverage systems.

Build capacity: A public billing authority

We could demonstrate the advantages of a public program within the current insurance system by way of a public authority assuming some of the responsibilities of private health insurance and operating at a lower cost. By mandating that all providers submit bills to a single public agency we could simplify billing for providers, establishing a universal set of codes and a single electronic billing system that would finally realize the potential of electronic medical records. This system would also create a database for epidemiological research, fraud prevention, and the study of billing practices by different insurance providers. And it would build the infrastructure for Medicare for All.

Build capacity: Medicare for the very sick

Insurers currently buy reinsurance to protect themselves from unexpected costs. We could require them to buy this coverage from a public program which would assume the costs for enrollees spending over a specified amount. At $10,000 per person, for example, this reinsurance program would cover 5% of those with private health insurance coverage and over 50% of medical expenses. Such a program would put the public agency in a position to drive down prices by bargaining with providers, insisting, for example, that they accept Medicare prices.[15]

Demonstrate viability and build capacity: Let Medicare compete—Medicare for all who want it

Because of its greater efficiency, Medicare could be offered to the general population at a lower price than most private insurance.[16] This would save money for enrollees and force competing health insurers to lower costs, thereby demonstrating the benefits of government involvement and promoting alliances with employers and others burdened by high insurance premiums.[17]

Demonstrate viability and build capacity: Midlife Medicare and KiddieCare

Lowering the age for Medicare and providing Medicare to children were part of the original vision of Medicare's advocates.[18] Both children and the near elderly are ripe for public programs. If they lose their job, older workers often find it difficult to find employment because of the cost of health insurance, and find that it is very expensive to buy on the individual market. The cost of insuring the young and the elderly also distorts competitive markets because employers face higher costs if they have many older workers or many with family coverage.[19]

Demonstrate viability and reach out for allies: Accept cost-sharing

Advocates of Medicare for All have insisted on quality insurance coverage without even co-pays or deductibles, but there is a widespread concern that universal care free at the point of service will lead to an explosion in demand for services.[20] I oppose cost-sharing. It raises administrative costs and violates the principle of universal access with all the benefits in health and social cohesion that brings.[21] I also believe that critics of Medicare overstate the savings from cost-sharing. Nonetheless, it would be easier to establish a public program with some limits on coverage and some cost-sharing, as has been the practice everywhere else in the world.[22] We could eliminate cost-sharing and institute comprehensive coverage later, after having established the program.

Setting cost-sharing at the level of a gold rating on the Affordable Care Act exchange—at an actuarial value of 90%, rather than the ultra-platinum level envisioned in current Medicare for All legislation—would lower spending by 5% and provide revenue from deductibles and co-pays so that the need for tax revenue would fall by over a third. If we raised deductibles, co-pays, and other forms of cost-sharing to the level of the current Medicare program, the additional tax revenue required would drop to less than $250 billion. This could be financed with an increase in the Medicare payroll tax rate from 2.9% to 5.9%, at a cost of about $15 a week for the typical employee.[23]

Demonstrate viability:
Universal insurance at the state level

There are active campaigns to establish state-level universal coverage programs in 18 states, campaigns energized by disappointment at the lack of progress on the national level.[24] While state programs would be limited, they could demonstrate the possibility of an efficient and effective program for Medicare for All.

Disarm the opposition: Buy our opponents
Providing compensation to those who have profited from illness and disability is an idea that some may find repugnant. It would help to win an enactment, however, if we could reduce opposition. And to achieve this we should compensate health insurers and owners of for-profit health facilities.

Based on the market value of ten large health insurers—companies that account for over half of the market in the United States—it would cost around $1 trillion to buy the entire US health insurance industry.[25] While one might regard this as an exorbitant, even extortionate price, it could also be seen as a bargain if this initial investment of $1 trillion leads to annual savings of $200 billion in insurance industry administrative waste, along with comparable or even larger savings from investments in buying hospitals, drug companies, and others.

Taking Politics Seriously

For over 70 years, activists have abandoned the campaign for universal, publicly funded health insurance in order to seek limited reforms within the private health insurance system. Only once did activists combine practical political energy with a resolute commitment to universal care. The result was Medicare and Medicaid, after Robert Ball and his associates seized a political moment and did not hesitate to use conservative means to achieve liberal ends.[26] No one has done as much since. Maybe it's past time for us to return to their model.

For decades, the campaign for Medicare for All has been led by crusaders for whom an action is sometimes judged by its intrinsic virtue rather than by what it accomplishes. But lawmaking is a matter for neither an academic seminar nor a Bible class.[27] Effective politics requires a strategy to build a majority among opposing viewpoints; it involves the hard work of coalition building, negotiation, even appeasement. We must mobilize our natural supporters but also demonstrate to others the viability and superiority of our position. The opposition to Medicare for All is well funded, well organized, and has a clear message and plan. It is time for us to catch up. Medicare for All needs to become a campaign, not a crusade.

4

Universal Healthcare Is Better Economics Because It Acknowledges Human Rights

We hold these truths to be self-evident, that all men are created equal, that they are endowed by their Creator with certain unalienable Rights, that among these are Life, Liberty, and the pursuit of Happiness.

Human Rights and the Market for Healthcare

Can a nation pledged to the self-evident truths of equal and "unalienable Rights" make these rights depend on income? How can we reconcile these rights with using markets to distribute essentials, such as healthcare? This is the central issue for many activists: they reject the use of markets because they believe that we all have a human right to the means to maintain our lives, liberty, and well-being.[1] This makes such activists an easy target for critics who would present themselves as rational pragmatists, conscious of the tragic necessity of market allocation as essential for work incentives and economic efficiency.

Since Jefferson and the Continental Congress wrote these words in 1776 we have made great strides in extending equal rights, so much so that a recent American president was comfortable proclaiming that the arc of the moral universe "bends towards justice."[2] We have emancipated slaves, extended the vote as well as legal equality to all adults, and established welfare and taxation programs that have dramatically reduced inequality. All these gains were achieved through hard political struggle and are maintained only through continued vigilance.

Yet disparities remain. At best, our practice remains inconsistent with our values; at worst, it mocks our founders' noble sentiments. As the economist Arthur Okun wrote in a famous address in 1975:

> American society proclaims the worth of every human being. All citizens are guaranteed equal justice and equal political rights. Everyone has a pledge of speedy response from the fire department

and access to national monuments. As American citizens, we are all members of the same club.

Yet at the same time, our institutions say "find a job or go hungry," "succeed or suffer." . . .

Such is the double standard of a capitalist democracy, professing and pursuing an egalitarian political and social system and simultaneously generating gaping disparities in economic well-being. This mixture of equality and inequality sometimes smacks of inconsistency and even insincerity.[3]

Okun might have added, we say "succeed in the marketplace or you will be denied the healthcare you need to live."

The quotation from Okun highlights how advocates and critics of Medicare for All talk past each other. A prominent liberal Democrat, Okun defended our continued reliance on markets over rights as a tragic compromise rather than deliberate insincerity. Every extension of rights risks undermining work incentives: the more people are guaranteed, the less incentive they have to work hard and be efficient, and the poorer we will all be. There is a trade-off between the equal right to pursue happiness and society's ability to provide the means for this happiness.

In highlighting the economic cost of rights, Okun articulated what has become a popular view among economists, leading many to defend unregulated markets as essential for economic efficiency. Accepting a sad truth, they argue that we must sacrifice some of our idealism and our commitment to human rights because rights come at the risk of generalized poverty.

This approach has been extended to the debate over Medicare for All. While some critics dispute whether there should be any right to life, liberty, and the pursuit of happiness, most prefer to emphasize the economic argument that Medicare for All would cost too much and would discourage work effort.[4] Advocates who respond by asserting universal human rights, insisting that no one should die because they cannot afford healthcare, implicitly cede this economic argument. Presenting themselves as well-meaning but impractical idealists, they allow their critics to maintain a hardheaded and responsible posture.

It is ironic, then, that the stronger economic case is for rights rather than markets. Nearly a half-century of economic research has found little evidence to support Okun's trade-off, and much reason to dismiss it.[5] Rising levels of inequality not only promote social discontent and lower average happiness, they also undermine efficiency by lowering worker morale and effort, discouraging cooperation, raising transaction costs, and reducing the development of human capital. The strong economic performance of European countries with much larger social welfare programs should demonstrate the compatibility of these with economic efficiency. By promoting feelings of solidarity and commitment, and improving education and training, rights can be productive. And it can be reliance on markets and incentives that makes us poor.

The lesson we can draw from this economic debate is that, as a nation, we could provide healthcare more efficiently and enjoy a more efficient economy if we treated healthcare as a right. Because a humane society is inherently more productive, we can live by our values as well as enjoy prosperity. We can live better and longer.

Economists Against Healthcare

It is said that economists know the price of everything but the value of nothing. This makes them the original purveyors of Wendell Potter's FUD triumvirate of fear, uncertainty, and doubt. A decent and humane man, Okun based his argument about equality and efficiency on fear: the fear that individuals will exploit the generosity of the public; the doubt and uncertainty that anything can be gained by helping others.

Perhaps it is time that we started to doubt the economists' pronouncements. They have been wrong again and again about healthcare.[6] They were wrong about the effect of market incentives on efficiency within the healthcare system. And, in the campaign against Medicare for All, their efforts to defend for-profit industry healthcare have led to almost absurd arguments. High prices for drugs? Necessary to give drug producers incentives for research and development. High administrative costs? Necessary to control fraud and overutilization. High billing and insurance-related expenses within provider offices? Regrettable, but these would be even worse under a national single-payer system. High provider prices? Not the result of market power, but necessary to give providers an incentive to work hard.[7]

The Efficiency of Rights

There is a larger point at issue here. Critics of Medicare for All operate on the common assumption that the attitudes shaping conduct and the talents people bring to the economic system are independent of policy. Regardless of how society treats them, people come as they are, honest or criminal, kind or ruthless. This assumption of exogenously determined talents and preferences allows us to set incentives to encourage or to discourage behaviors without regard for any boomerang effect. Social policy works in only one direction, guiding behavior, but not shaping motivations.

To articulate this assumption is to condemn it. Society does more than set parameters; it shapes values. A decent society depends on people behaving responsibly and with consideration for others. We depend on what Alexis de Tocqueville called "self-interest properly understood." These values are taught by parents and communities. Good parents raise their children to be honest and to respect others. Neighbors, community leaders, and celebrities set examples, good or bad. And communities promote or discourage behavior by how they treat people, all with economic consequences.

Values matter. Honesty and a readiness to cooperate make it easier to maintain an efficient economy, promote trade, and encourage work by maintaining a clear connection between productive activity and income. Good moral values lower what economists call "transaction costs," the costs of establishing and maintaining property rights and economic exchanges.[8] If individuals are narrowly self-interested, then grifting or stealing usually make more sense than hard work. Such behavior, of course, not only drains energy from productive activity, but the requirement for additional guard labor to protect against theft and grifting wastes resources.[9]

Rights are productive because good moral values are the product of good treatment, treatment that goes beyond the family to basic state policy. We learn to treat others as we have been treated, at home, at work, and in our community. Raised to be ruthless, we accept ruthlessness as proper; treated with generosity and kindness, we respond in kind. When everything is for sale, we look to buy everything and seek to get richer than others so we can buy more. Sheltered from some of the shocks of flesh and life, we can treat others with similar generosity.

If we want people to behave well, be honest, and respect others, then we need social policies that show respect and caring for all. This is the great economic advantage that rights give democratic societies: universal citizenship that produces social welfare policies; good treatment that encourages the good values that support an efficient society. We can almost see the last century as a social experiment in the benefits and costs of market inequality. Throughout the Western world, the spread of egalitarian social welfare and tax policies in the mid-twentieth century lowered income disparities and created a more equal distribution of income.[10] Contradicting the expectations of those schooled on Okun's work, these policies were broadly productive and were associated with rising productivity and national well-being. Beginning in the 1970s in the United States and then in Britain and elsewhere, many countries abandoned their commitment to egalitarian welfare programs. The result has been not only rising inequality, but slower productivity and income growth.[11] Beyond lower incomes, greater inequality and an impersonal disregard for the well-being of individuals has led to declining social well-being.[12]

Treated poorly, told that society has no concern for their well-being beyond their capacity to earn, people react selfishly and in ways that undermine social cohesion and economic efficiency. We have seen this in recent decades, and across countries pursuing different social welfare policies. Distrust, drug abuse, theft, violent crime: these all rise with the reliance on unregulated markets and soaring inequality. There is an economic cost here in lost productivity, increased rates of incarceration, and the employment of more guard labor to protect property. Businesses experience these costs every day in lower employee morale and productivity as well as greater theft and security expenditures.[13] People respond to how they are treated and, shown due care and respect, they respond in kind. We are poorer because people have responded in kind to the disrespect shown them by a society organized around the market.

Values to Live By

Written by an economist, this work has focused on the economic case for Medicare for All. This can be misleading, however, because inefficiency may be the least important problem that arises from treating healthcare as a commodity. The greater issue is how it violates our fundamental values in a democratic community where we should all be treated with respect. Marketizing a fundamental need says that we are independent agents who live or die according to our ability to extract value from others. It denies that we are citizens of a Commonwealth. In a world where everything, even life, is for sale, we are without connection to each other, having no responsibilities and no bond except a cash nexus.

While we might warn that this type of competitive world will produce a toxic sense of alienation from society and from each other, that is exactly the world envisioned by economists and others who deny the social value of human rights. Is this what we want? Do we want a society where we are constantly out to gain advantage over others?

Empirically, the evidence is that we do not. People value community connections and want the security that comes from a relatively equal distribution of income and abundant social supports.[14] Man, as Aristotle taught, is a social animal. We live in cooperation and in social relationships with others. To treat people as participants in an impersonal marketplace is to deny a truth basic to our well-being. Societies with higher levels of inequality, societies that organize themselves around competitive markets, are less happy. Social support, trust, and generosity, all strongly associated with happiness, are all at risk when we treat our society as a giant marketplace. All are enhanced by social protections like universal healthcare.

This, therefore, is the larger issue, one going beyond economic efficiency or even subjective well-being. As a nation, as a community, we have pledged ourselves to recognize the intrinsic value of each person. Honoring this pledge is not restricted to when it is convenient. Our commitment to equal rights, to "life, liberty, and the pursuit of happiness," comes without equivocation. Neither the Declaration of Independence nor the Constitution limits the respect of these rights to "when it is economically efficient," or even "when it raises the average level of subjective well-being." We formed a "more perfect union" to ensure these rights for all Americans and to "promote the general welfare." All of us are members of our community, one formed to ensure that everyone has the opportunities that can be realized only with decent access to healthcare.

Medicare for All will save money and make the United States a richer and happier country because it marks a step away from the universal marketization of our lives. It is a policy consistent with our values and with our national ethos. We know that it is the right thing to do; we are only waiting for a political movement and strategy.

Let us begin.

Notes

1 Craig Idlebrook, "Selling a Lifetime of Insulin for $3," *Insulin Nation* (blog), August 7, 2015, https://insulinnation.com/treatment/medicine-drugs/selling-lifetime-insulin; Stephen Eaton Hume, *Frederick Banting: Hero, Healer, Artist* (XYZ: Montreal, 2001).

2 Xinyang Hua et al., "Expenditures and Prices of Antihyperglycemic Medications in the United States: 2002–2013," *JAMA* 315, no. 13 (April 5, 2016): 1400–2.

3 William T. Cefalu et al., "Insulin Access and Affordability Working Group: Conclusions and Recommendations," *Diabetes Care* 41, no. 6 (June 2018): 1299–311; T1International, "Access Survey—T1International," https://www.t1international.com/insulin-and-supply-survey.

4 Tod Cooperman, "20 Drugs That Cost a Lot Less Outside the U.S.," *Huffington Post* (blog), December 1, 2017, https://www.huffingtonpost.com/entry/20-dru gs-that-cost-a-lot-less-outside-the-us_us_5a217e73e 4b0545e64bf9277.

5 Micaela Marini Higgs, "The High Price of Insulin is Literally Killing People," *Tonic* (blog), April 5, 2017, https://tonic.vice.com/en_us/article/ezwwze/the-high-price-of-insulin-is-literally-killing-people.

6 On November 18, 2018, there were 2,594,728 active solicitations for medical assistance. Reaching over 90% of his goal, Boyle did better than average. A sample from among the most successful ("trending") postings finds that these relatively successful campaigns raised less than 75% of their goal and fewer than a third reach their goal. Obviously, even fewer successes would be found among all postings.

7 Rachel Bluth, "GoFundMe CEO: 'Gigantic Gaps' in Health System Showing Up in Crowdfunding," *Kaiser Health News* (blog), January 16, 2019, https://khn.org/news/gofundme-ceo-gigantic-gaps-in-health-system-showing-up-in-crowdfunding.

8 Ibid.

9 Stuart H. Altman and David Shactman, *Power, Politics, and Universal Healthcare: The Inside Story of a Century-Long Battle* (Amherst, NY: Prometheus Books, 2011); Paul Starr, *Remedy and Reaction: The Peculiar American Struggle over Healthcare Reform* (New Haven: Yale University Press, 2011).

10 Medicare covers only 50% of healthcare spending by the elderly and Medicaid covers another 10%. The

remaining 40% must be covered by private health insurance or out-of-pocket spending.

11 See Steffie Woolhandler et al., "Proposal of the Physicians' Working Group for Single-Payer National Health Insurance," *JAMA* 290, no. 6 (August 13, 2003): 798–805; a good review of various proposals is Jodi L. Liu and Robert H. Brook, "What Is Single-Payer Healthcare? A Review of Definitions and Proposals in the U.S.," *Journal of General Internal Medicine* 32, no. 7 (July 1, 2017): 822–31; an excellent discussion can be found in Deborah Stone, "Single Payer—Good Metaphor, Bad Politics," *Journal of Health Politics, Policy and Law* 34, no. 4 (August 2009): 531–42.

12 See, for some examples, CAP Health Policy Team, "Medicare Extra for All," *Center for American Progress* (blog), https://www.americanprogress.org/issues/healthcare/reports/2018/02/22/447095/medicare-extra-for-all; Ezekiel J. Emanuel, *Healthcare, Guaranteed: A Simple, Secure Solution for America* (New York: PublicAffairs, 2008).

13 In 2013, less than half of healthcare spending in the United States was by government or compulsory programs, compared with 80% in other affluent countries. For a discussion of healthcare elsewhere, see Eric C. Schneider et al., "Mirror, Mirror 2017: International Comparison Reflects Flaws and Opportunities for Better U.S. Healthcare," Commonwealth Fund, 2017, http://www.commonwealthfund.org/interactives/2017/july/mirror-mirror/?omnicid=EALERT1243408&mid=gfriedma@eco

ns.umass.edu; Theodore R. Marmor, ed., *Whither Healthcare Policy? U.S., Canadian, and European Perspectives*, Canadian-American Public Policy, no. 51 (Orono, ME: Canadian-American Center, University of Maine, 2002).

14 Lee Miller and Wei Lu, "These Are the World's Healthiest Countries," *Bloomberg*, February 24, 2019, https://www.bloomberg.com/news/articles/20 19-02-24/spain-tops-italy-as-world-s-healthiest-nat ion-while-u-s-slips.

15 World Health Organization, "World Health Organization Assesses the World's Health Systems," https://www.who.int/whr/2000/media_centre/press_ release/en.

16 OECD, "OECD Health Statistics 2018," http:// www.oecd.org/els/health-systems/health-data.htm.

17 Central Intelligence Agency, "The World Factbook— Central Intelligence Agency," https://www.cia.gov/ library/publications/the-world-factbook.

18 Institute of Medicine (US) Committee on the Consequences of Uninsurance, "Estimates of Excess Mortality Among Uninsured Adults," 2002, http:// www.ncbi.nlm.nih.gov/books/NBK220638.

19 Pricivel M. Carrera, Hagop M. Kantarjian, and Victoria S. Blinder, "The Financial Burden and Distress of Patients with Cancer: Understanding and Stepping-up Action on the Financial Toxicity of Cancer Treatment," *CA: A Cancer Journal for Clinicians* 68, no. 2 (2018): 156.

20 By contrast, only 6% in other high-income countries rationed insulin, and 17% rationed test strips;

T1International, "Costs and Rationing of Insulin and Diabetes Supplies: Findings from the 2018 T1International Patient Survey," June 18, 2019, https://www.t1international.com/media/assets/file/ T1International_Report_-_Costs_and_Rationing_of _Insulin__Diabetes_Supplies_2.pdf.

21 These figures are from the Medical Expenditure Panel Survey for 2017; given the trend in these results, it is likely that the numbers are higher today. Agency for Healthcare Research and Quality, "Medical Expenditure Panel Survey," 2017, http://www.meps. ahrq.gov/mepsweb/data_stats/state_tables.jsp?region id=18&year=-1.

22 Federal Reserve Board of Governors, "Dealing with Unexpected Expenses," https://www.federalreserve. gov/publications/2019-economic-well-being-of-us-households-in-2018-dealing-with-unexpected-expen ses.htm.

23 Carrera, Kantarjian, and Blinder, "The Financial Burden and Distress of Patients with Cancer," 157.

24 Schneider et al., "Mirror, Mirror 2017." This is much larger than the number who died because they lacked health insurance because it includes all barriers to access. With gaps in coverage, co-pays, and deductibles, the Commonwealth Fund estimates that 45% of US adults aged 19 to 64 are inadequately insured; see Sara Collins, Herman Bhupal, and Michelle Doty, "Health Insurance Coverage Eight Years after the ACA: Fewer Uninsured Americans and Shorter Coverage Gaps, But More Underinsured," survey brief, Commonwealth Fund, February 2019, https://

www.commonwealthfund.org/sites/default/files/20
19-02/Collins_hlt_ins_coverage_8_years_after_AC
A_2018_biennial_survey_sb.pdf.

25 Martin Gaynor, Farzad Mostashari, and Paul B.
Ginsburg, "Making Health Care Markets Work:
Competition Policy for Healthcare," Center for
Health Policy at Brookings, April 2017, 4, https://
www.brookings.edu/wp-content/uploads/2017/04/
gaynor-et-al-final-report-v11.pdf.

26 The share of consumers with medical debt is taken
from William E. Bruhn et al., "Prevalence and
Characteristics of Virginia Hospitals Suing Patients
and Garnishing Wages for Unpaid Medical Bills,"
JAMA, June 25, 2019. While Himmelstein and
others exaggerate, bankruptcy is serious: David U.
Himmelstein et al., "Medical Bankruptcy in the
United States, 2007: Results of a National Study,"
The American Journal of Medicine 122, no. 8
(August 1, 2009): 741–46; Carlos Dobkin et al.,
"Myth and Measurement—The Case of Medical
Bankruptcies," *New England Journal of Medicine*,
March 22, 2018, https://www.nejm.org/doi/10.10
56/NEJMp1716604; Javier Valero-Elizondo et al.,
"Financial Hardship From Medical Bills Among
Nonelderly U.S. Adults With Atherosclerotic
Cardiovascular Disease," *Journal of the American
College of Cardiology* 73, no. 6 (February 19, 2019):
727–32. Over a 40-year period, as many as one in
five Americans will go bankrupt because of medi-
cal debt; United States Courts, "Bankruptcy Filings
Continue to Decline," April 26, 2018, https://www.

uscourts.gov/news/2018/04/26/bankruptcy-filings-continue-decline.

27 James E. Dalen and Joseph S. Alpert, "Medical Tourists: Incoming and Outgoing," *The American Journal of Medicine* 132, no. 1 (January 1, 2019): 9–10; Rachel Bluth, "Faced With Unaffordable Drug Prices, Tens of Millions Buy Medicine Outside U.S.," *Kaiser Health News* (blog), December 20, 2016, https://khn.org/news/faced-with-unaffordable-drug-prices-tens-of-millions-buy-medicine-outside-u-s.

28 Patients Beyond Borders, "Medical Tourism Statistics & Facts," July 12, 2011, https://patientsbeyondbord ers.com/medical-tourism-statistics-facts.

29 Canada's model began as hospital insurance in Saskatchewan in the 1950s under the premiership of Tommy Douglas, grandfather of Kiefer Sutherland. By 1971 it had been extended to all provinces and to physician costs under what became known as Medicare. In 2004, a public survey by a Canadian TV show declared Douglas the greatest Canadian.

30 Gerard F. Anderson et al., "It's the Prices, Stupid: Why the United States is So Different From Other Countries," *Health Affairs* 22, no. 3 (May 1, 2003): 89–105; Zack Cooper et al., "The Price Ain't Right? Hospital Prices and Health Spending on the Privately Insured," December 2015, https://www.nber.org/papers/w21815; Sarah Kliff, "The Problem is the Prices," *Vox*, October 16, 2017, https://www.vox.com/policy-and-politics/2017/10/16/16357790/hea lth-care-prices-problem.

31 Progressive Party, "Progressive Party Platform of

1912," The American Presidency Project, https://www.presidency.ucsb.edu/documents/progressive-party-platform-1912.

32 Committee on Economic Security, "Report to the President of the Committee on Economic Security: Final Report on Risks to Economic Security Arising out of Ill Health," March 7, 1935, https://www.ssa.gov/history/reports/health.html.

33 Franklin Roosevelt, "State of the Union Address, January 11, 1944," Franklin D. Roosevelt Presidential Library and Museum, http://www.fdrlibrary.marist.edu/archives/address_text.html.

34 Stuart D. Brandes, *American Welfare Capitalism, 1880–1940* (Chicago: University of Chicago Press, 1976); Sanford M. Jacoby, *Modern Manors: Welfare Capitalism since the New Deal* (Princeton: Princeton University Press, 1997); Jennifer Klein, *For All These Rights: Business, Labor, and the Shaping of America's Public-Private Welfare State* (Princeton: Princeton University Press, 2003).

35 The tax exemption for employer-provided benefits goes back to 1913 but the explicit exemption for employer-provided health insurance dates to 1943; see Congressional Budget Office, "The Tax Treatment of Employment-Based Health Insurance," Congressional Budget Office, March 1994, https://www.cbo.gov/sites/default/files/103rd-congress-1993-1994/reports/1994_03_taxtreatmentofinsurance.pdf.

36 Robert M. Ball, "What Medicare's Architects Had in Mind," *Health Affairs* 14, no. 4 (January 1,

1995); Theodore Marmor and Jonathan Oberlander, "Medicare at 50," January 2018, https://www.res earchgate.net/publication/320036193_Medicare_at_ Fifty.

37 The American Presidency Project, "1960 Democratic Party Platform," https://www.presidency.ucsb.edu/ documents/1960-democratic-party-platform.

38 David Blumenthal, Karen Davis, and Stuart Guterman, "Medicare at 50—Origins and Evolution," January 14, 2015, http://www.commonwe althfund.org/publications/in-the-literature/2015/ jan/medicare-at-50-origins-and-evolution?omnicid= EALERT676115&mid=gfriedma@econs.umass.edu.

39 Altman and Shactman, *Power, Politics, and Universal Healthcare.*

40 Starr, *Remedy and Reaction.*

41 Jonathan Gruber and Benjamin D. Sommers, "The Affordable Care Act's Effects on Patients, Providers and the Economy: What We've Learned So Far," NBER, June 2019, https://www.nber.org/papers/ w25932.

42 Sherry A. Glied and Adlan Jackson, "Access to Coverage and Care for People with Preexisting Conditions: How Has it Changed Under the ACA?," Commonwealth Fund, June 22, 2017, http://www. commonwealthfund.org/publications/issue-briefs/ 2017/jun/coverage-care-preexisting-conditions-aca? omnicid=EALERT1230884&mid=gfriedma@econs. umass.edu.

43 Congressional Budget Office, "The Distribution of Household Income, 2014," United States Congress,

Congressional Budget Office, March 2018, https://www.cbo.gov/system/files/115th-congress-2017-2018/reports/53597-distribution-household-income-2014.pdf.

44 For just one good example, see John P. Geyman, *Hijacked: The Road to Single Payer in the Aftermath of Stolen Healthcare Reform* (Monroe: Common Courage Press, 2010).

45 Kaiser Family Foundation, "Cost-Sharing for Plans Offered in the Federal Marketplace for 2019," *The Henry J. Kaiser Family Foundation* (blog), December 5, 2018, https://www.kff.org/health-reform/fact-she et/cost-sharing-for-plans-offered-in-the-federal-mar ketplace-for-2019.

46 Center for Medicaid and Medicare Statistics, "National Health Expenditure Projections 2017–2026," Centers for Medicare & Medicaid Services, Office of the Actuary, n.d., https://www.cms.gov/Research-Statistics-Data-and-Systems/Statistics-Tre nds-and-Reports/NationalHealthExpendData/Natio nalHealthAccountsProjected.html.

47 Another view critical of the ACA from a different perspective is John C. Goodman, *Priceless: Curing the Healthcare Crisis*, Independent Studies in Political Economy (Oakland, Calif: Independent Institute, 2012).

48 Diane Archer, "Medicare is More Efficient Than Private Insurance," *Health Affairs* (blog), http://healthaffairs.org/blog/2011/09/20/medicare-is-more-efficient-than-private-insurance; Diane Archer and Theodore Marmor, "Medicare And Commercial

Health Insurance: The Fundamental Difference," *Health Affairs* (blog), February 15, 2012, http://health affairs.org/blog/2012/02/15/medicare-and-commer-cial-health-insurance-the-fundamental-difference/comment-page-1/#comment-165108.

49 Medicare Payment Advisory Commission, "A Data Book: Healthcare Spending and the Medicare Program," June 2018, 11, http://www.medpac.gov/docs/default-source/data-book/jun18_databookenti rereport_sec.pdf.

50 For critics, see, for example, John Davidson, "50 Years Later, Medicaid and Medicare Still Spend Us Into Oblivion," *The Federalist*, July 31, 2015, http://thefederalist.com/2015/07/31/medicare-medicaid-same-problems-50-years-ago. A better approach is found in David U. Himmelstein and Steffie Woolhandler, "Cost Control in a Parallel Universe: Medicare Spending in the United States and Canada," *Archives of Internal Medicine* 172, no. 22 (December 10, 2012): 1764–6.

51 Martin S. Feldstein, "The Welfare Loss of Excess Health Insurance," *Journal of Political Economy* 81, no. 2 (1973): 251–80; John C. Goodman and Gerald L. Musgrave, *Patient Power: Solving America's Healthcare Crisis* (Washington, DC: Cato Institute, 1992).

Chapter 1

1 Kenneth J. Arrow, "Uncertainty and the Welfare Economics of Medical Care," *The American*

Economic Review 53, no. 5 (December 1, 1963): 941–73; Amy Finkelstein, *Moral Hazard in Health Insurance: Developments since Arrow (1963)*, Kenneth J. Arrow Lecture Series (New York: Columbia University Press, 2014).

2 Paul Starr rightly notes how institutional features of American medicine contribute to the information asymmetries emphasized by Arrow; see Starr, *The Social Transformation of American Medicine* (New York: Basic Books, 1982), 225–7.

3 As Starr noted, institutional design contributes to the effect of information on market power. For pharmaceuticals, see the effect of patent law discussed in Dean Baker, "A Free Market Solution for Prescription Drug Crises," *International Journal of Health Services: Planning, Administration, Evaluation* 34, no. 3 (2004): 517–26.

4 Michael D. Frakes, Jonathan Gruber, and Anupam Jena, "Is Great Information Good Enough? Evidence from Physicians as Patients," Working Paper (National Bureau of Economic Research, July 2019), https://doi.org/10.3386/w26038.

5 For example, Cleveland Clinic advertises on NPR; New York Presbyterian advertises at the New York Yankees.

6 David Dranove and Mark Satterthwaite, "The Industrial Organization of Healthcare Markets—Northwestern Scholars," in *Handbook of Health Economics*, vol. 1 (Amsterdam and New York: Elsevier, 2000), 1093–139, https://www.scholars.northwestern.edu/en/publications/chapter-20-the-

industrial-organization-of-health-care-markets. In 2001, when PacificCare insurance refused to accept the rates demanded by St. Joseph's Hospital system in Orange County, it quickly had to back down when subscribers shifted their coverage to other insurers in order to maintain access to the St. Joseph system. People care more about maintaining access to providers than they do about their insurance company. Joseph White, "Markets and Medical Care: The United States 1993–2005," *Milbank Quarterly* 85, no. 3 (2007): 424.

7 For this reason, there is no insurance market for cosmetic surgery or other entirely elective procedures.

8 Deborah Stone, "Values in Health Policy: Under standing Fairness and Efficiency," 2014, https://policyparadox.files.wordpress.com/2014/11/values-in-health-policy-understanding-fairness-and-efficiency-with-eye-witness-section.pdf.

9 David A. Moss, *When All Else Fails: Government as the Ultimate Risk Manager* (Cambridge, MA: Harvard University Press, 2002).

10 Council of Economic Advisers, "Opportunity Costs of Socialism," Council of Economic Advisers, October 2018, 9–10, https://www.whitehouse.gov/wp-content/uploads/2018/10/The-Opportunity-Costs-of-Socialism.pdf.

11 See, for example, the role of Obama's economists in the fight over the MLR rule in the ACA, discussed in Starr, *Remedy and Reaction*; the economists' focus on moral hazard over adverse selection is discussed in Finkelstein, *Moral Hazard in Health Insurance*.

12 Uwe E. Reinhardt, "JAMA Forum: Where Does the Health Insurance Premium Dollar Go?," *News@ JAMA* (blog), April 25, 2017, https://newsatjama. jama.com/2017/04/25/jama-forum-where-does-the-health-insurance-premium-dollar-go.

13 Archer, "Medicare is More Efficient Than Private Insurance"; Kip Sullivan, "How to Think Clearly About Medicare Administrative Costs: Data Sources and Measurement," *Journal of Health Politics, Policy and Law* 38, no. 3 (June 1, 2013): 479–504.

14 Steffie Woolhandler, Terry Campbell, and David Himmelstein, "Cost of Healthcare Administration in the United States and Canada," *New England Journal of Medicine*, no. 349 (2003): 768–75.

15 Emily Gee and Topher Spiro, "Excess Administrative Costs Burden the U.S. Healthcare System," Center for American Progress, April 8, 2019, https://cdn. americanprogress.org/content/uploads/2019/04/03 105330/Admin-Costs-brief.pdf.

16 Aliya Jiwani et al., "Billing and Insurance-Related Administrative Costs in United States' Healthcare: Synthesis of Micro-Costing Evidence," *BMC Health Services Research* 14, no. 556 (2014), http://www. biomedcentral.com/content/pdf/s12913-014-0556-7. pdf; Steffie Woolhandler and David Himmelstein, "Administrative Work Consumes One-Sixth of U.S. Physicians' Working Hours and Lowers Their Career Satisfaction," *International Journal of Health Services* 44, no. 4 (January 1, 2014): 635–42. A California study found that physician practices spend over 40% of their cost on bill processing and other

administrative tasks; James G. Kahn et al., "The Cost Of Health Insurance Administration in California: Estimates for Insurers, Physicians, and Hospitals," *Health Affairs* 24, no. 6 (November 1, 2005): 1629–39.

17 Bonnie B. Blanchfield et al., "Saving Billions Of Dollars—And Physicians' Time—By Streamlining Billing Practices," *Health Affairs* 29, no. 6 (2010), https://www.healthaffairs.org/doi/10.1377/hlthaff. 2009.0075.

18 Starr, *Remedy and Reaction*.

19 Matt Bruenig, "People Lose Their Employer-Sponsored Insurance Constantly," April 4, 2019, https://www.peoplespolicyproject.org/2019/04/04/ people-lose-their-employer-sponsored-insurance-con stantly.

20 For a recent study of the role of insurance provider networks in ACA Exchange Plans, see Physicians for Fair Coverage, "The High Cost of Healthcare: Patients See Greater Cost Shifting and Reduced Coverage in Exchange Markets 2014–2018," July 2018, https://www.endtheinsurancegap.org/research-shows-high-patient-costs-less-access-care. For a study of the frequency and medical impact of interruptions in insurance coverage, see Mary A. M. Rogers et al., "Interruptions in Private Health Insurance and Outcomes in Adults With Type 1 Diabetes: A Longitudinal Study," *Health Affairs* 37, no. 7 (July 1, 2018): 1024–32; Jay Hancock, "Churning, Confusion and Disruption—The Dark Side Of Marketplace Coverage," *Kaiser Health News* (blog), December 7,

2017, https://khn.org/news/churning-confusion-and-disruption-the-dark-side-of-marketplace-coverage; Christiaan J. Lako, Pauline Rosenau, and Chris Daw, "Switching Health Insurance Plans: Results from a Health Survey," *Healthcare Analysis* 19, no. 4 (December 2011): 312–28.

21 Anderson et al., "It's the Prices, Stupid."

22 The Veterans Administration pays prices close to world levels, half what the rest of us pay. See Austin Frakt, Steven D. Pizer, and Roger Feldman, "Should Medicare Adopt the Veterans Health Administration Formulary?," SSRN Scholarly Paper (Rochester, NY: Social Science Research Network, April 14, 2011), http://papers.ssrn.com/abstract=1809665; International Federation of Health Plans, "2013 Comparative Price Report: Variation in Medical and Hospital Prices by Country," https://www.federal reserve.gov/publications/2019-economic-well-being-of-us-households-in-2018-dealing-with-unexpected-expenses.htm; US Department of Health and Human Services, "Comparison of U.S. and International Prices for Top Spending Medicare Part B Drugs", October 25, 2018, https://aspe.hhs.gov/system/files/pdf/259996/ComparisonUSInternationalPricesTop SpendingPartBDrugs.pdf.

23 Jared Maeda and Lyle Nelson, "An Analysis of Hospital Prices for Commercial and Medicare Advantage Plans," Congressional Budget Office, June 26, 2017, https://www.cbo.gov/system/files/115th-congress-2017-2018/presentation/52819-pres entation.pdf.

24 Office of Massachusetts Attorney General Martha Coakley, "Investigation of Healthcare Cost Trends and Cost Drivers," January 29, 2010, https://www.mass. gov/files/documents/2016/08/ub/prelim-2010-hcct cd.pdf; Nicholas C. Petris Center on Healthcare Markets and Consumer Welfare, "Consolidation in California's Healthcare Market 2010–2016: Impact on Prices and ACA Premiums," School of Public Health, University of California, Berkeley, March 26, 2018, http://petris.org/wp-content/uploads/2018/ 03/CA-Consolidation-Full-Report_03.26.18.pdf; Daria Pelech, "An Analysis of Private-Sector Prices for Physician Services," Congressional Budget Office, June 26, 2017, https://www.cbo.gov/system/files/ 115th-congress-2017-2018/presentation/52818-dp-presentation.pdf; Robert Kocher and Nikhil R. Sahni, "Hospitals' Race to Employ Physicians—The Logic Behind a Money-Losing Proposition," *New England Journal of Medicine* 364, no. 19 (May 12, 2011): 1790–93.

25 Ge Bai and Gerard F. Anderson, "A More Detailed Understanding of Factors Associated With Hospital Profitability," *Health Affairs* 35, no. 5 (May 1, 2016): 889–97.

Chapter 2

1 "'Medicare for All' Could Cost $32.6 Trillion, George Mason Study Says," *Time*, July 30, 2018, http://time.com/5352950/medicare-trillions-bernie-sanders; Charles Blahous, "The Costs of a National

Single-Payer Healthcare System," Mercatus Center, July 25, 2018, https://www.mercatus.org/publica tions/federal-fiscal-policy/costs-national-single-pay er-healthcare-system.

2 Seema Verma, "CMS BLOG: Medicare for All? Just Another Name for a Government-Run, Single Payer System," November 2, 2018, https://www.cms.gov/ blog/cms-blog-medicare-all-just-another-name-gove rnment-run-single-payer-system.

3 Ibid.

4 Jonathan Yates, "A Single-Payer System Will Cause the Healthcare Sector to Implode," *Des Moines Register*, July 31, 2018, https://www.desmoinesregi ster.com/story/opinion/columnists/iowa-view/2018/ 07/27/single-payer-system-cause-health-care-sector-implode/849329002.

5 Ibid. For a review of the media coverage, see Justin Anderson, "Reporting on Bernie Sanders' 'Medicare for All' is Deeply Flawed: Media Forgets How Math Works," *Salon*, August 3, 2018, https://www.salon. com/2018/08/03/reporting-on-bernie-sanders-medica re-for-all-is-deeply-flawed-media-forgets-how-math-works.

6 There would remain an independent, privately financed sector for those who, for whatever reason, reject the public program and refuse to accept free healthcare. For the most part, however, there will be only one bill payer.

7 Reduced burnout will also lead to significant financial savings for the healthcare system. See Shasha Han et al., "Estimating the Attributable Cost of

Physician Burnout in the United States," *Annals of Internal Medicine* 170, no. 11 (June 4, 2019): 784.

8 Shira Tarlo, "We Asked Experts What Healthcare Would Look Like Under Medicare for All," *Salon*, July 14, 2019, https://www.salon.com/2019/07/14/this-is-what-doctor-visits-would-look-like-under-medicare-for-all.

9 Roosa Tikkanen and Robin Osborn, "Does the United States Ration Healthcare?," Commonwealth Fund, July 11, 2018, https://www.commonwealthfund.org/blog/2019/does-united-states-ration-health-care.

10 Schneider et al., "Mirror, Mirror 2017."

11 Canada uses its MRIs and CT scanners more intensively than does the United States; OECD, "OECD Health Statistics 2018"; Robert G. Evans, *Strained Mercy: The Economics of Canadian Healthcare* (Toronto: Butterworths, 1984).

12 Schneider et al., "Mirror, Mirror 2017."

13 Jacob S. Hacker and Paul Pierson, *American Amnesia: How the War on Government Led Us to Forget What Made America Prosper* (New York: Simon & Schuster, 2016).

14 Nancy Yu, Zachary Helms, and Peter Bach, "R&D Costs For Pharmaceutical Companies Do Not Explain Elevated US Drug Prices," *Health Affairs* (blog), March 7, 2017, https://www.healthaffairs.org/do/10.1377/hblog20170307.059036/full.

15 Donald W. Light and Rebecca Warburton, "Demythologizing the High Costs of Pharmaceutical Research," *BioSocieties* 6, no. 1 (March 1, 2011): 34–50.

16 Donald Light and Joel Lexchin, "Pharmaceutical Research and Development: What Do We Get For All That Money?," *British Medical Journal*, August 11, 2012.

17 Andrew Joseph, "'A Blizzard of Prescriptions': Documents Reveal New Details About Purdue's Marketing of OxyContin," *STAT* (blog), January 15, 2019, https://www.statnews.com/2019/01/15/massachusetts-purdue-lawsuit-new-details.

18 Roger Collier, "Drug Patents: The Evergreening Problem," *Canadian Medical Association Journal* 185, no. 9 (June 11, 2013): E385–6.

19 Robin Feldman, "May Your Drug Price Be Ever Green," UC Hasting Research Paper, University of California Hastings College of the Law, June 13, 2018, https://papers.ssrn.com/abstract=3061567.

20 Every country with national health insurance has some form of cost-sharing.

21 S. H. Cheng and T. L. Chiang, "The Effect of Universal Health Insurance on Healthcare Utilization in Taiwan: Results from a Natural Experiment," *JAMA* 278, no. 2 (July 9, 1997): 89–93; Philip E. Enterline et al., "The Distribution of Medical Services Before and After Free Medical Care—The Quebec Experience," *New England Journal of Medicine* 289, no. 22 (November 29, 1973): 1174–8.

22 Amanda Frost and David Newman, "Spending on Shoppable Services in Healthcare," Healthcare Cost Institute, March 2016, https://www.healthcost institute.org/images/easyblog_articles/110/Shoppable-Services-IB-3.2.16_0.pdf.

23 For a review of estimates, see Josh Katz, Kevin Quealy, and Margot Sanger-Katz, "Would 'Medicare for All' Save Billions or Cost Billions?," *New York Times*, April 10, 2019, https://www.nytimes.com/in teractive/2019/04/10/upshot/medicare-for-all-bernie-sanders-cost-estimates.html.

24 Gregory Pope et al., "Risk Transfer Formula for Individual and Small Group Markets Under the Affordable Care Act," *Medicare & Medicaid Research Review* 4, no. 3 (2014): E1–23.

25 Cathy Schoen, Karen Davis, and Amber Willink, "Medicare Beneficiaries' High Out-of-Pocket Costs," Commonwealth Fund, May 12, 2017, https://www.issuelab.org/resources/27426/27426.pdf; Tara Siegel Bernard, "'Too Little Too Late': Bankruptcy Booms Among Older Americans," *New York Times*, August 6, 2018, https://www.nytimes.com/2018/08/05/busi ness/bankruptcy-older-americans.html.

26 This is in addition to the $20 trillion already committed to federal health programs, notably Medicare and Medicaid. An additional $4 trillion in tax expenditure subsidies for employer-provided health insurance would become available in additional federal revenues. I am also assuming maintenance of effort by the states for the Medicaid program at existing nominal values for an additional $2.5 trillion over ten years.

27 These estimates are all discussed in greater depth in Gerald Friedman, "Yes, We Can Have Improved Medicare for All," Business Initiative for Health Policy, December 11, 2018, https://businessinitiative.

org/wp-content/uploads/2019/01/We-Can-Have-Im
proved-M4A-Friedman-ilovepdf-compressed.pdf.

Chapter 3

1 Loss aversion, where people fear losses more than they value prospective benefits, is discussed in Dan Ariely, *Predictably Irrational: The Hidden Forces That Shape Our Decisions*, (New York: Harper, 2008).

2 As an ad executive at CIGNA in the 1990s, Potter himself helped to devise the FUD campaign that undermined the Clinton healthcare initiative. See Wendell Potter, *Deadly Spin: An Insurance Company Insider Speaks Out on How Corporate PR is Killing Healthcare and Deceiving Americans* (New York: Bloomsbury Press, 2010); Wendell Potter, "Don't Let $418 Million of FUD Fool You," October 17, 2014, http://wendellpotter.com/2014/10/dont-let-41 8-million-of-fud-fool-you.

3 Brendan Gill, "Ad Spending Trends in Pharma and Healthcare," *Extreme Reach* (blog), July 24, 2018, https://extremereach.com/blog/ad-spending-trends-in-pharma-and-healthcare.

4 Medical Marketing and Media, "50 Celebrity Healthcare Endorsements," February 9, 2016, https://www.mmm-online.com/home/channel/campa igns/50-celebrity-healthcare-endorsements.

5 Sarah Hand, "Shire Launches Second Dry Eye Disease Awareness Campaign Featuring Jennifer Aniston," *Xtalks*, January 11, 2018, https://xtalks.

com/shire-launches-second-dry-eye-disease-awaren ess-campaign-featuring-jennifer-aniston-1075.

6 Open Secrets, "Lobbying Spending Database," https://www.opensecrets.org/lobby/top.php?indexTy pe=i.

7 Open Secrets, "Health Services/HMOs," https:// www.opensecrets.org/industries/indus.php?ind=H03 ++.

8 Marcia Angell, *The Truth About the Drug Companies: How They Deceive Us and What to Do About It*, revised and updated edition (New York: Random House, 2005).

9 Jane Mayer, *Dark Money: The Hidden History of the Billionaires Behind the Rise of the Radical Right* (New York: Doubleday, 2016); Nancy MacLean, *Democracy in Chains: The Deep History of the Radical Right's Stealth Plan for America* (New York: Viking, 2017).

10 The Commonwealth Fund is usually the most politi-cally progressive of the research bodies and has a broader range of opinions represented on its board. In addition to four members with industry experi-ence, there are three with research credentials and two with experience in program management, including a former director of the UK National Health Service.

11 See, for example, the discussion at the National Economic and Social Rights Initiative, "Parroting The Right: How the Media's and Polling Companies' Repetition of Insurance-Industry Framing Mani-pulates Public Opinion," https://parrotingtheright. org.

12 Finkelstein, *Moral Hazard in Health Insurance.*

13 In addition, there were two scholarship and fellow-ship programs, a program on the effect of a four-day school week policy in rural areas, and support for IT to link health data with scholars.

14 Baker, "A Free Market Solution for Prescription Drug Crises."

15 This could be done at the state level as well as nation-ally.

16 See Jacob S. Hacker, *Health at Risk: America's Ailing Health System—and How to Heal It* (New York: Columbia University Press, 2012).

17 Medicare would have to be upgraded to compete because the current program has a relatively low actuarial value and limited benefits; see CAP Health Policy Team, "Medicare Extra for All."

18 Marmor and Oberlander, "Medicare at 50."

19 Extending Medicare in this way would require the infusion of public funds into a program that has in the past been almost entirely self-supporting. At current Medicare spending rates, adjusted for age, it would cost approximately $96 billion and $30 billion for the near elderly and the young respectively, offset by Medicare premiums of $17 billion for those 55–64 and $19 billion for the under-18 population.

20 See, for example, Stuart H. Altman, "The Detail That Could Make Medicare for All Generous—and Expensive," *Axios*, https://www.axios.com/medica re-for-all-out-of-pocket-costs-7aa80feb-ea06-4f35-a 43a-9cfc719ab897.html; John Holahan et al., "The Sanders Single-Payer Healthcare Plan: The Effect

on National Health Expenditures and Federal and Private Spending," Urban Institute, Health Policy Center, May 2016, http://www.urban.org/sites/def ault/files/alfresco/publication-pdfs/200785-The-San ders-Single-Payer-Health-Care-Plan.pdf; Jodi L. Liu and Christine Eibner, "National Health Spending Estimates Under Medicare for All," https://www.ra nd.org/pubs/research_reports/RR3106.html; Dylan Matthews, "Kenneth Thorpe's Analysis of Bernie Sanders's Single-Payer Proposal," *Scribd*, January 27, 2016, https://www.scribd.com/doc/296831690/ Kenneth-Thorpe-s-analysis-of-Bernie-Sanders-s-sing le-payer-proposal.

21 Deborah Stone, "Beyond Moral Hazard: Insurance is Moral Opportunity," *Connecticut Insurance Law Journal* 6, no. 1 (1999): 11–46.

22 On cost-sharing in foreign countries, see Schneider et al., "Mirror, Mirror 2017"; for alternative models, see Katz, Quealy, and Sanger-Katz, "Would 'Medicare for All' Save Billions or Cost Billions?"

23 Gerald Friedman, "'Medicare for All' Could Be Cheaper Than You Think," *The Conversation*, http://theconversation.com/medicare-for-all-could-be-cheaper-than-you-think-81883.

24 See the list at https://www.healthcare-now.org/legisla tion/state-single-payer-legislation/

25 This is almost 50% higher than the estimate given by Van Der Wege and Gottlieb, largely reflecting the run-up in health insurance share prices over the last few years. See Eldon Van Der Wege and Thomas Gottlieb, "U.S. Healthcare Financing Reform: The

Consolidation of the Health Insurance Industry," Healthcare for All Colorado Foundation, March 27, 2017, http://d3n8a8pro7vhmx.cloudfront.net/themes/57508665cd0af5cf9d000001/attachments/original/1490687208/2017.03.27-Healthcare-Financing-Article.pdf.

26 Ball, "What Medicare's Architects Had In Mind"; Edward D. Berkowitz, *Robert Ball and the Politics of Social Security* (Madison: University of Wisconsin Press, 2003); Julian E. Zelizer, *The Fierce Urgency of Now: Lyndon Johnson, Congress, and the Battle for the Great Society* (New York: Penguin, 2015).

27 Max Weber, "Politics as a Vocation" (1919), http://anthropos-lab.net/wp/wp-content/uploads/2011/12/Weber-Politics-as-a-Vocation.pdf.

Chapter 4

1 Arthur M. Okun, *Equality and Efficiency: The Big Tradeoff* (Washington: Brookings Institution, 1975); Gøsta Esping-Andersen, *The Three Worlds of Welfare Capitalism* (Princeton: Princeton University Press, 1990); Charles Edward Lindblom, *Politics and Markets: The World's Political Economic Systems* (New York: Basic Books, 1977).

2 Martin Luther King Jr., and after him Barack Obama, condensed and misquoted Theodore Parker. For the original, see Theodore Parker, *The Present Aspect of Slavery in America and the Immediate Duty of the North: A Speech Delivered in the Hall of the State House, before the Massachusetts Anti-Slavery*

Convention, on Friday Night, January 29, 1858 (Boston: Bela Marsh, 1858).

3 Okun, *Equality and Efficiency*, 1.

4 The development of the conservative critique of liberal social policies is discussed in MacLean, *Democracy in Chains*.

5 Richard G. Wilkinson, *The Spirit Level: Why Greater Equality Makes Societies Stronger* (New York: Bloomsbury Press, 2010); David Alex, "Inequality is Fracturing American Democracy and Killing Prosperity," *Evonomics* (blog), May 27, 2017, http:// evonomics.com/inequality-fracturing-democracy-killing-prosperity-david-alexander; A. B. Atkinson, *Inequality: What Can Be Done?* (Cambridge, MA: Harvard University Press, 2015); Danny Dorling, "The Equality Effect: Improving Life For Everyone," http:// www.dannydorling.org/?p=6034; Paul Krugman, "Inequality Is a Drag," *New York Times*, August 7, 2014, http://www.nytimes.com/2014/08/08/opinion/ paul-krugman-inequality-is-a-drag.html.

6 They were also wrong about the financial markets leading up to the great recession of 2008. But that is another story.

7 Council of Economic Advisers, "Opportunity Costs of Socialism," 47–51.

8 The concept was first propounded in economics by R. H. Coase, "The Nature of the Firm," *Economica* 4, no. 16 (November 1, 1937): 386–405.

9 John Joseph Wallis and Douglass C. North, "Should Transaction Costs Be Subtracted From Gross National Product?," *The Journal of Economic*

History 48, no. 3 (1988): 651; Samuel Bowles, *The Moral Economy: Why Good Incentives Are No Substitute for Good Citizens* (New Haven: Yale University Press, 2016); Samuel Bowles and Herbert Gintis, "Productivity-Enhancing Egalitarian Policies," *International Labour Review* 134, no. 4/5 (1995): 559–85; Francis Fukuyama, *Trust: The Social Virtues and the Creation of Prosperity* (New York: Free Press, 1995).

10 Thomas Piketty, *Capital in the Twenty-First Century*, trans. Arthur Goldhammer (Cambridge, MA: Harvard University Press, 2014).

11 Robert J. Gordon, *The Rise and Fall of American Growth: The U.S. Standard of Living Since the Civil War* (Princeton: Princeton University Press, 2016); David M. Gordon, *Fat and Mean: The Corporate Squeeze of Working Americans and the Myth of Managerial "Downsizing"* (New York: Martin Kessler Books, 1996).

12 John Helliwell, Richard Layard, and Jeffrey D. Sachs, "World Happiness Report, 2018," 2018, https://s3.amazonaws.com/happiness-report/2018/WHR_web.pdf.

13 Wilkinson, *The Spirit Level*; Alex, "Inequality is Fracturing American Democracy and Killing Prosperity"; Guglielmo Barone and Sauro Mocetti, "Inequality and Trust: New Evidence from Panel Data," Temi di discussione (Economic working papers), Bank of Italy, Economic Research and International Relations Area, 2014, https://ideas.repec.org/p/bdi/wptemi/td_973_14.html. Comparative

international studies find positive happiness and well-being associated with greater equality in the distribution of income and greater social welfare services. See Helliwell, Layard, and Sachs, "World Happiness Report, 2018"; and "The Stark Relationship between Income Inequality and Crime," *The Economist*, June 7, 2018, https://www.economist.com/graphic-detail/2018/06/07/the-stark-relationship-between-income-inequality-and-crime.

14 Helliwell, Layard, and Sachs, "World Happiness Report, 2018." The negative association between social alienation and well-being is an old idea in social theory. See Emile Durkheim, *Suicide: A Study in Sociology* (London: Routledge & Kegan Paul, 1952).